VALUOCITY III

Breaking Free from Solo Practice

Books by Dr. Marc Cooper & Dr. Mark Silberg

Valuocity: A Fable for Dentists

Valuocity II: Meanwhile Back at the Office

Books by Dr. Marc B. Cooper

Mastering the Business of Practice
Not a 'How To' Book but a 'Who To' Book

Partnerships in Dental Practice
Why Some Succeed and Why Some Fail

SOURCE
The Genesis of Success in Business & Life

Running on Empty
Answers to Questions Dentists have about the Recession
(with Chris Creamer)

The Elder
(with James Selman)

VALUOCITY III

Breaking Free from Solo Practice

Dr. Marc Cooper

Chris Creamer

VALUOCITY III
Breaking Free from Solo Practice

*Text Copyright © 2015 by
Dr. Marc B. Cooper and Chris Creamer*

All Rights Reserved.

*Published by Sahalie Press
Woodinville, Washington*

No part of this publication may be reproduced in whole or in part, or stored in a retrieval system, or transmitted in any form or by any means, electronic, mechanical, photocopying, recording or otherwise, without permission in writing from the publisher, except by a reviewer who may quote brief passages in a review. For longer quotations, permission requests may be addressed to: Sahalie Press, P.O. Box 1806, Woodinville, WA, 98072, USA.

ISBN: 978-1981720248

Library of Congress Control Number: 2015902367
CreateSpace Independent Publishing Platform
North Charleston, SC

Printed in the U.S.A.

First Edition, 2015

Editing by Matt King

INTRODUCTION
The Decline of Solo Practice

The evidence is undeniable. Solo private practice, except in the most highly branded concierge practices, is an unsustainable model to meet the conditions of the future. There are a number of forces shaping the future that are unfavorable to solo private practice and very conducive to managed group practice.

According to the ADA, in 2008, 76% of all dental practices were solo. By 2010 that number had dropped to 69%. Using standard analysis, the trend line results in solo practices being less than 50% of the industry by 2020 and some are saying it could be closer to 20% in time. What is beginning to fill that void is managed group practice.

Dental school tuition is increasing and the typical graduating dentist now emerges with educational debt of $300,000 to $400,000. With this mountain of debt, it makes it much tougher to purchase existing practices. Banks are also becoming tougher lenders to young dentists, fearful that practice revenues will not make them good risks. Whereas, managed group practices are typically well financed, giving them much greater capacity for purchasing existing practices.

Senior dentists are not offering dental graduates associateships. The senior doctor's constant refrain is, "You need five years of experience." In addition, most established solo dentists don't have enough patients to support both an associate and themselves. Without private practice associateships available, one of the few alternatives for young graduates is to work for a managed group practice to get experience and their debt paid down. By the end of five years they will have achieved a strong personal income, significantly reduced their student debt, and might be able to buy stock in the company without putting themselves at much risk.

The ADA Health Resource Institute (2014) reports that practice revenues, patient visits, numbers of new patients, patient expenditures per procedure have gone flat and are trending downward. While the expenses of running a practice, with constant upgrades in technology, continue to increase at a much greater pace than inflation. Expenses are climbing faster than revenues. Managed group practices, because of their economies of scale, can afford to purchase new technology as well as hold the line on expenses because of their leverage in negotiations.

Seventy three percent of patients seen in a dental office have some form of dental plan. Ninety-two percent of dentists take patients with some form of plan. Insurance companies are now 80 percent PPO and, therefore, control the fees. In a PPO environment, where the fees are reduced by twenty-percent or higher, sustaining a sufficient level of revenue in solo dental practice is getting harder and harder, whereas managed group practice can thrive in a reduced fee environment.

The Affordable Health Care Act mandates that plans participating in the Exchange must offer dental care to children under 18. How will solo private practice handle this? They can't. But managed group practices can.

Trends in health care reimbursements are beginning to focus on values and outcomes, which include quality assurance, and these will be overlaid on dentistry by the end of the decade. Peer review, chart review, algorithms for treatment planning, risk assessment and risk management, disease management will become strong components in dentistry. How will solo practice handle these forces? They can't. Solo practice is based on a fee-for-service model or pay-for-procedure. Managed group practices can establish structures and supply additional personnel to address quality assurance.

Goldman Sachs, other large capitalists, equity partners and major banks believe that managed group practice in dentistry is a very strong investment. Billions (not millions) of capital is now flowing into the market to consolidate practices. The money is not aimed at solo practice, but at managed group practice. Significant capital will flow into dentistry to generate managed group practices fueling their growth.

According to the ADA, by the end of the decade 47% of graduating dental students will be women who commonly do not want to own, but rather practice on a limited basis. A solo practice needs full time providers, managed group practices do not.

According to Malcolm Gladwell, the tipping point occurs between fifteen and eighteen percent of market share. The growth of managed group practice will soon surpass the tipping point.

This conclusion is further supported by the 80/20 rule which always prevails. Given the rapid growth of managed group practices and the decline of solo practice, it is our belief that the majority of dentistry will be delivered by managed group practice within a decade.

Consolidation of providers and their practices has occurred in medicine, pharmacy, podiatry, veterinary and optical. Dentistry will follow this path. It is inevitable. This book was written for the dentist in solo practice who realizes the future of solo practice is coming to an end and wants to know how to make the transition into the new world of managed group practice.

The train is leaving the station. My recommendation is that you get on board.

PROLOGUE

Though the conversation had occurred nearly five years earlier, Carl Oldquist remembered vividly the scene as he and his wife, Veronica, drove back from Chicago after Carl's workshop with Sidney Kaprov and Frank Chemento.

"Penny for your thoughts?" Veronica asked as Carl merged onto I-90.

Carl glanced over at his wife and smiled. "A penny a thought? I'd make a fortune right now. I've got a million thoughts after that workshop."

"Well, in that case, I'll just take a nickel's worth." Veronica dug into her purse, took a nickel out and dropped it in Carl's cup holder. "Okay, Let's hear it. What's on your mind?"

Carl made a show of retrieving Veronica's nickel and pretending to bite it to see if it was real. "One can never be too careful with city slickers, you know."

"I have no idea what you mean, Dr. Oldquist. I'm just a country girl from Madison."

"Country bred, but city smart. However, since you value my thoughts so highly, I'll give you your money's worth." He plunked the nickel back into his cup holder. *"As always, after talking with Sidney and Frank, I feel optimistic. Like I understand and can see the road forward with the practice.*

"I think I really get their message of vision, mission and purpose and how it comes from a commitment to core values. I see that I need to be a stronger owner, leader and manager, and, with Sidney and Frank's coaching I feel like I've started to improve in those roles."

"You have," Veronica interrupted. *"You did a very difficult think in firing Sharon, but you did it for the good of the practice. You've got the rest of the staff agreeing on a set of core values. And that's all happened in two weeks!"*

"I know. We've taken some big steps." Carl paused. "I guess that's what's really on my mind. In some ways, making changes is easy. It's whether they are the right changes and, if they are, how to sustain them. It's those next steps that weigh on me now."

"If those next steps, even if they are small ones, are in the right direction then we'll be good," Veronica added optimistically. "And we are going in the right direction. I really liked how Sidney and Frank got us focused on the purpose of our practice. You are in this business to provide good dental care for patients. It's about our patients' well-being. Just thinking about it from that angle re-energized me to work the front desk next week."

Carl reached over and patted Veronica's hand. "You're right about that. That sense of purpose is powerful and if we can get the rest of the staff thinking along those lines and make our goals clear enough, it will really build our sense of mission. And we can rally around that and be a better team."

"That's what I'm talking about!" Veronica playfully punched his arm. "I think that was a nickel well spent."

"Yeah. Now, I'm tempted to invest a bit more to see the inner workings of one Veronica Oldquist."

"Oh, save your money. I'm pretty transparent." Veronica admitted. "I think you see right through me."

"Just to your heart of gold."

The rest of their drive to Madison was a content one—on a smooth road that held a clear path forward.

CHAPTER 1

Carl clearly remembered the feeling of clarity that day. He and Veronica were both galvanized around rebuilding the practice on their core values. And they had. Day by day. Month by month. Year by year. They had invested the time to make their core values the foundation in the running of the practice: customer service and patient care. The practice had not only rebounded, it had flourished.

That's why Carl felt so lost on this Tuesday evening, staring at his numbers on the monitor in his private office. The overhead lights were off and the staff had gone home. All the busy-ness of the day had died away—along with his sense of well-being.

Carl was reeling from the numbers on the screen in front of him. Slowly scrolling through the line items he witnessed the downward trend. A growing despondency was settling in his gut like a lead brick. Carl continued to stare, looking for some insight, some sign of what he could do to stem the bleeding. Everything was turning red on his bottom line.

He hadn't felt this crushing weight since the crash of 2008 when his practice had taken a nosedive. He had struggled mightily to recover his financial footing and it was only by chance—or providence—that he had met Dr. Sidney Kaprov at the ADA meeting in San Antonio along the River Walk. He swiveled away from the disheartening spreadsheet on his computer, leaned back and closed his eyes, remembering that warm October day in 2009 when he'd walked out of the Henry B. Gonzales Convention Center with the hope that fresh air and a change of scenery would magically help him solve the problems with his practice. It was then that he had run into Sidney.

Sidney had turned out to be a sage, and in many ways a savior. Following a trip to his Taos ranch and learning the value of core values, purpose and mission, as well as the power of coaching with Frank Chemento, Carl had been able to stop his practice's financial slide in relatively short order and returned to a successful path of growth and prosperity.

Things had been very good, in fact. Veronica had partnered with him in rebuilding the practice and they talked regularly about where things were heading. But, that positive growth had begun to ebb, and was now evaporating before his eyes. The office was running efficiently, standards were high and staff was fully behind the vision. So, why the slippage? Why the current hemorrhaging of patients and production?

Opening his eyes, Carl returned his attention to the monitor. He opened his latest practice performance reports. He had asked Denise, his office manager who had replaced Sharon five years ago, to e-mail him a one-page practice performance report for the last year. Clearly, the practice had gone flat—was actually, in fact, contracting. The report confirmed that new patients were down to single digits. Case acceptance was south of fifty percent and procedures that were being accepted by patients were the most minimal care possible. Total patient visits were down as well as recall visits.

Carl's mind spun. *I'm doing everything I know to do: team meetings, reinforcing core values, talking about the vision and the mission. I'm sure our SOPs are being followed. I've got Demand Force in place. I've got Kari promoting us on Facebook. We're asking patients to refer. We've opened additional hours on Thursday evenings and Fridays. I've squeezed every dime I can out of overhead expenses.*

Carl took a deep breath to calm himself. As he looked again at the performance report he could see that it hadn't been a rapid decline, but more like a very slow drip. Until last year the numbers of new patients, the level of case acceptance and gross production had been increasing faithfully at a healthy 12-15 percent annually. Staff was in great shape. He had felt more like a leader than ever before. His morning huddles, his once-a-month staff meetings, and the sense of team, it was all there. Goals were set and met.

Tonight, reviewing the reports, the practice felt more like a rocket that had run out of fuel and, feeling the pull of gravity, was now plummeting back to Earth. Carl had sensed the lack of momentum for several months, but now he could see it in the numbers.

He had once had a strong foundation of fee-for-service patients, but many of them had become more cost conscious of late, asking, "Do you take my insurance?" He started to worry that patients would leave if he didn't. When he finally signed up with several insurance companies, he was forced to join their PPOs, which knocked at least twenty percent right off the top.

In the beginning he was able to compensate for the PPO write-offs by increasing efficiencies, reducing costs and working harder. He attended courses on how to increase fee-for-service patients, but whatever the leaders were talking about in these courses wasn't the reality in which his practice was operating. His market just wasn't looking to spend money on their teeth. He had a family practice, not a cosmetic-reconstructive practice. Mostly blue collar patients, not Wall Street hedge fund folks.

Making matters worse, several corporate dental offices had sprung up around him. Smile Right Now, a regional player with fifteen offices and a national chain, Stratford Dental, with 200 practices nationwide had offices within 10 miles. These corporate 'blue meanies' had acquired some of the better practices in town which really worried Carl. Many of the doctors Carl had known for years.

At their local Seattle Study Club meeting and the state association meeting Carl had inquired as to why they'd sold. The answers were nearly the same. *Money was right. Tired of managing. Solid exit strategy.*

His questions often went deeper into what they liked and didn't like about being part of a corporation. Dr. Joe Campbell, a friend from dental school, who started his practice the same time as Carl, had told him, "I miss the autonomy I used to have. I can't do what I want, when I want. Management decisions are made by the management company and some of those decisions I don't agree with. But they leave me alone when it comes to diagnosing and treatment planning, so I can do the dentistry I want to do. Honestly, it is a lot easier. I just go to work and do my dentistry. I don't have to do all that other stuff to make the practice work and the money in the end, with cash and stock, is going to be better."

More and more, as Carl spoke with colleagues about corporate dentistry, he wondered if it was an option for him. He thought about Smile Right Now's offices. They all looked the same, with their light and dark blue exteriors with chrome accents, the Smile Right Now name in large brushed metal silver letters and their oval logo. He had to admit the offices looked attractive, even eye catching. Smile Right Now heavily promoted their services and locations on TV, radio and in print ads.

Both Smile Right Now and Stratford Dental had lots more money to spend on marketing compared to Carl. He simply couldn't afford TV, radio and billboards. These corporations were also competing directly on price, posting fees for exams, X-rays, cleaning, implants and crowns in their ads. They were a lot less than Carl charged. If Carl charged the same fees he wouldn't be able to pay his bills.

This was Carl's growing competition and his spreadsheets told him he was losing the game. That made him think of Sidney Kaprov. Sidney had often used sports analogies, especially basketball, to help Carl understand what happens when you are prepared. For a basketball shooter in his groove the rim looks big. Carl could feel his world and his practice shrinking. He needed the rim to look big again.

At his ranch in Taos, Sidney had taken Carl through the process of basing his practice on core values, generating an authentic vision, having a driving purpose, working on his culture and communication, firing people who didn't belong and hiring people who did, generating plans and goals. He had helped Carl reimagine what was possible and given him the tools to reformulate his practice.

He needed that mojo again. He hadn't spoken to Sidney in years. He'd followed him online and run into him at a couple conferences, but once Sidney (and Frank) had helped get him over the hump five years ago, he hadn't stayed in touch.

Reluctantly, he picked up his cell-phone and searched his contacts for Sidney. When he saw it in his directory, he hesitated. Was it a sign of weakness to reach out when things got tough? Years ago, Sidney had convinced him that it was not. Still, he wondered if this was the right move.

But he couldn't think of anything else to do.

Carl tapped Sidney's name and the phone came to life and began dialing. His heart raced, hoping like he had back in San Antonio so long ago that Sidney wouldn't pick up.

CHAPTER 2

"Hello, this is Sonia, how can I help you?"

Carl didn't recall anyone named Sonia and hesitated.

"Hello?" Sonia asked again. "Is anyone there?"

Feeling embarrassed, Carl momentarily thought about hanging up, but then mustered his courage and replied, "Sorry, I am trying to reach Dr. Kaprov. Is this the right number?"

"Yes, this is his number. I am Dr. Kaprov's personal assistant. Can I help you?"

"Oh, I didn't know he had an assistant," remarked Carl.

"Well, he just got so busy over the last couple years he needed someone to keep his appointments and calendar in order. What can I do for you?"

"Well, I'm Dr. Carl Oldquist, a former client of Dr. Kaprov's and I was hoping to speak with him."

"Oh sure. Sidney's out on the north part of the property with his ranch manager. We've got a coyote problem and we've been losing some livestock."

"Is Richard still the ranch manager?" Carl asked thinking about the enigmatic Native American who mystified him with koans that always sank deep.

Sonia laughed lightly. "Sure is. In fact, Richard's my brother-in-law. That's how I got my job. The ranch just kept getting busier and busier. More calls. More visitors. More work than ever before. Richard told

Sidney he needed help and suggested he consider a personal assistant. And so here I am."

"I assume Dawn is still there, too. She is the best cook."

"Yes, she is and she still keeps folks here happy with her menus. If you've worked with Sidney you know he is all about values. And, believe me, he values a hearty meal and so he bends over backward to keep Dawn happy."

"That I remember well. Sonia, I'm just hoping I can arrange to speak with Sidney sometime soon."

"Is it an urgent matter?"

Carl hesitated, not wanting to sound desperate, yet realizing his situation was getting precarious and he wouldn't be sleeping well until he could get some answers. He bit the bullet and laid it out for Sonia. "Well, the situation is urgent to me. My practice has run into a bit of a crisis. Sidney helped me out five years ago and I'm hoping he can provide some guidance."

"I understand, Dr. Oldquist. Let me look at Sidney's schedule this evening." She paused. "It looks like he should be able to give you a call at 7:30, if that will work for you."

Carl let out a long exhalation realizing he'd been holding his breath while Sonia checked the calendar. "That's fantastic. I'd really appreciate being able to talk to him tonight, but I don't want to be an imposition."

"Don't worry, Dr. Oldquist."

"Please call me, Carl."

"Sure, Carl. Don't worry about the timing. Sidney believes that his clients are clients for life. He likes to keep up with people, and with former clients he likes to know if he made a difference."

"Well, I wouldn't be calling now if he hadn't made a huge difference five years ago."

"That's good to hear. Okay, I've got you up on the screen. You want Sidney to call you at home?"

"That would be perfect."

"Great then. I'll have Sidney call you at home at 7:30."

"Thanks so much, Sonia. I see that service at the ranch is still top notch. I appreciate your time and concern. Have a good evening."

"You too, Carl. My husband, Robert, who is Richard's brother, and I are going to a local rodeo later. Robert rides, so I'm hoping it's not too bumpy a night for him."

"Well, best of luck to you both tonight. Goodbye and thanks again."

"You're very welcome."

Carl ended the call. He was happy that he'd reached out to Sidney and Sonia had made him feel welcome. He needed that boost, because although he wasn't getting on a bucking bronco like Sonia's husband, he sensed that he might have a very wild and potentially dangerous ride ahead in dealing with the downturn in his practice.

At least, he thought, as he logged off his computer, grabbed his things and headed out into the chill of the February evening, he had some help coming. Not exactly the cavalry, but Sidney Kaprov might be the next best thing.

CHAPTER 3

His mind was racing as fast as the car's wheels were spinning; Carl tried to map out what he would say to Sidney. He also knew he had to explain to Veronica why he'd scheduled this call tonight.

It wasn't like five years ago when he'd blindsided his wife with the news that the practice was in deep trouble. He shared a lot more with Veronica these days and she was fully involved in the business of their practice. She knew business had been flat for a while, but like Carl, she had assumed it would be temporary. Now Carl had the most recent metrics and he needed to share his deep misgivings about the current path they were on.

In one thing, though, he was confident. Veronica was the consummate can-do person. Their last crisis with the practice had revealed this in spades. Veronica could step up to the plate and get things done. That was a powerful thing knowing she had his back. He pulled into his driveway about 6:30 feeling he had a lot to do.

As he opened the door into the house from the garage, he could smell garlic and onions. *Italian tonight*, he thought and hoped it was Veronica's incredible lasagna. Veronica was in the kitchen setting the table for two.

"Hey, honey," Carl said as he walked over to give Veronica a peck on the lips. Her auburn hair was pulled tightly into a ponytail. She smiled; "Amy's at a friend's tonight studying for her calculus test tomorrow. Open some wine if you want. It's just the two of us."

That happened more and more often. With Jonathon off at college and Amy deep into high school activities, he and Veronica were getting an early taste of being empty nesters. That was a bit hard for him to get used to—but it more or less mirrored the change occurring in his practice. Change was the constant, whether he liked it or not.

Carl took off his jacket, put it over the back of a kitchen chair, took out his phone and placed it on the shelf next to the radiating Wolf oven.

Carl opened the utility drawer and pulled out an old-fashioned cork screw. As he began the task of uncorking the wine, he figured it was time to let Veronica know what was going on.

"Honey, you remember Sidney Kaprov. I called him before I left the office. I think we may need his help again. Things are just not rebounding like we'd hoped. He's calling at 7:30 and I'd like you on the call."

Veronica stopped what she was doing and asked, "It's not looking as bad as the last time, is it?"

"The numbers aren't as dismal, but the trend's not looking good." Crossing his arms, he leaned back against the counter, enjoying the warmth of the nearby stove. "The toughest part is that I know we've been doing things right. We're working harder and smarter and should be doing better—that's what's really eating at me."

Veronica winked. "Well, let's eat now and you can tell me what you're going to tell Sidney."

"We've weathered these storms much better because of your calm and common sense."

"I don't feel that calm inside," Veronica confessed. "It's scary to think this is happening again after all your hard work."

"All *our* hard work," he corrected.

"Well, it leaves me wondering what's going on in the world of dentistry that is making us so vulnerable."

Carl walked to the table. "Yeah. Let's put our heads together and puzzle this out so when Sidney calls we can give him some clues."

They ate and talked, attempting to understand their work and life together like millions of other couples on the earth that night. A comfort and a constant in a world of change.

CHAPTER 4

The phone interrupted the stillness at 7:30 on the nose. He and Veronica were sitting in their living room with a second glass of wine. Carl met Veronica's eyes as he picked up the wireless house phone from the coffee table. He put the phone on speaker and answered it deliberately. "Hello, this is Carl."

"Hello, Carl, this is Sidney. It's been a long time, my friend. How are you? How's Veronica? How are the kids?"

"Yes, it's been too long, Sidney, and that's my fault for not staying in better touch. The kids are great. Jonathon is a freshman at the University of Minnesota and Amy is a sophomore in high school. Veronica's right here with me. I've got you on speaker."

"Hello then, Veronica. How is Carl's better half?"

Veronica chuckled. "I'm well—or at least half as well as Carl. Thanks for asking, Sidney. How are you doing?"

"I'm doing good for an old rancher. Other than a bunch of coyotes harassing my livestock, I've got no complaints."

"Yeah," Carl said. "Your assistant Sonia told me that you and Richard were on it."

"Indeed. I only wish coyotes held the same values I do. Then we could set up a system of requests and promises. Ha!"

Carl laughed, remembering the meeting he'd attended five years ago where the senior ranch hands had dealt with problems using requests and promises. It seemed a world away. "Well, Sidney, if anyone can get coyotes to change their behaviors it might be you. In some ways it might be easier than working with dentists, eh?"

Sidney chuckled back. "You might be right about that, Carl. Especially with what's happening to dentistry. It's thick with predators these days. At least that's how dentists see it. I tend to look at it a bit more like climate change. The conditions and context of our profession are changing rapidly. And I'd wager that's what prompted your call?"

Carl smiled and looked to Veronica with a how-does-he-do-that expression.

"As always, Sidney, you are prescient. Veronica and I have seen the practice flatten out over the last year and now it's trending downward in a worrisome way. In spite of the management tools you helped us put in place five years ago, the practice is slipping."

"Okay, be specific. Let me get a clear picture of what's going on."

Carl took a deep breath and reported. "This last reporting period, all our numbers were down 15 to 20 percent, new patients, production, case acceptance. Hygiene is battling to stay at 70% return rate." He added that they had started taking third party insurance a couple years ago.

"I extended my hours. I am doing what worked in the past with morning huddles, staff meetings, individual and group acknowledgment. I revisit the core values often, use the language of commitment, and constantly talk about the purpose of the practice. But it's like wet firewood; I can't get things relit like before."

"Not for lack of trying," Veronica interjected.

"Veronica," Sidney asked, "What's your perspective on what's happening?"

"Carl has been very committed to running the practice according to our values of great care and service which revived us in 2008, but it doesn't seem to be enough. It appears that everything is being driven by price and insurance and we're having a hard time holding onto patients. Does that make sense?"

"Yes," Sidney replied and then paused for a moment before continuing. "Carl, Veronica, you are doing business the right way by basing your practice on your values. You're doing what you know produced results in the past. You're being good leaders and managers. So don't feel like it's something wrong with you or your approach. Nothing is wrong with you. Or with the thousands of other dentists like you who own practices. The bottom line is that what worked in the past isn't working as well now and won't work in the future."

"Sorry, Sidney, I don't understand," Carl said in alarm. "All the things we worked on—values, vision, communication—worked brilliantly. Why shouldn't a winning formula continue to work?"

"This is what is so difficult about what's going on. It's not about you and how your practice is being run. I used the example of climate change because it helps owners understand. You may have been able to grow tomatoes for years and years with great success, but suddenly the harvest begins to decline. You're using the best growing methods and giving the best care, but the plants aren't producing because the climate has changed. The fundamentals you were used to no longer apply. That's what's happening in dentistry, the economic climate, the business context has changed. And, as we know, context is decisive."

Sidney paused for a moment to let that sink in, then he asked, "Remember payphones? When was the last time you used one. In fact, when was the last time you even saw one?"

"A long time ago."

"What happened to payphones, something that many people used and even depended on for almost a century?" asked Sidney.

"Cell phones," Veronica answered. "Almost everybody has a phone with them all the time. No need for payphones."

"Exactly. That's what I mean when I say context is decisive. Once cell phones came out, the context of phone communication changed. Payphones became obsolete. Cell phones brought about a new context.

Context decides what succeeds and what fails. No matter how good the payphones were, in a context of cell phones they became obsolete. Same thing with sending letters through the postal service. Email, blogs, social media, Skype, the new context of digital communication. You can apply it to shopping as well. The Internet has changed the whole economic context of commerce."

"So, what's the new context of dentistry?" Carl asked anxiously.

"This may be difficult to hear, but it is my view that solo dental practice, like payphones, is not likely to survive in this new context."

Carl stared at Veronica in dead silence. He was stunned by Sidney's frank declaration. It was like his doctor telling him he had two years to live. Finally, he found his voice. "What's causing this change?"

"Think about it this way, Carl. How many physicians do you know who practice alone?"

After brief consideration, Carl offered, "Except for plastic surgeons, I don't know, maybe none?"

"Same with pharmacists and optometrists," Sidney added. "They're all in groups now. And just like in medicine, pharmacology and optometry, the group approach is the new context emerging in dentistry."

"But isn't dentistry different than medicine and those others?" Carl asked, feeling defensive.

"Not really," Sidney answered bluntly. "The same forces that caused physicians and opticians to join together are now present in dentistry. Maybe they're coming from different sources, but they are the same economic, political and social forces. Let me just run through a few of the causes: expenses to run a dental practice are increasing faster than inflation, revenues are decreasing per patient, insurance companies are now the decision maker, dentistry is more a commodity now, dental student debt is off the charts, capitalists see dentistry as a retail business, access is more difficult for people. These and other forces are quickly reshaping the context of dentistry."

"What do you suggest we do?" Veronica asked. Carl was reassured by her use of *we*.

"Well, if you want to learn more about what you're up against as a solo practice, I'd suggest you join me here in Taos in three weeks. I have a small group of dentists coming in for a Friday and Saturday workshop. These dentists are all in the same boat. Good practitioners with solid core values who care about their patients, but their practices are beginning to circle the drain. My recommendation is that you attend."

"What will the workshop cover?" Carl asked.

"What is happening in the dental industry, why it is happening, what is the likely future, and what dentists like yourself can do about it."

"Hang on a moment, Sidney, while Veronica and I discuss it."

"No need to," Veronica interrupted him. "Carl will be there. You helped us get back on our feet five years ago and I think we both know that you're our best bet now to figure out what's next."

Carl stared at his wife, smiling. That was Veronica. Ready to trust and act. Turning back to the phone he responded, "You heard her, Sidney. Looks like I'll see you in Taos."

"Great. I'll have Sonia contact you with all the details. She'll also send you a homework assignment to complete before the workshop."

"Homework?" Carl groaned jokingly.

"We're going to be diving into the new context of dentistry and this homework will help you get clearer on your local environment. Trust me, Carl, it'll be worth the work."

"I get it. And you know we trust you. That's why I called."

"I value your trust and I hope to continue to earn it when you come to Taos. Have a good evening. See you soon!"

"Thank you, Sidney," Veronica said as Carl ended the call.

"And thank *you*," Carl said to Veronica, "for being supportive and decisive."

"As Sidney says, *context is decisive*," Veronica cooed.

CHAPTER 5

The next morning when Carl arrived at his office, Sonia had already e-mailed the details for the workshop: instructions on travel, transportation to the ranch, clothing to bring, special food requirements, cell phone coverage, availability of WiFi, and a time schedule for the program.

Curiously though, Carl noticed, an agenda of topics was not listed, just the times with generic headings like Morning Session, Afternoon Break, etc. Carl wondered why he hadn't listed specific topics for each session. Must have his reasons, he thought. But he had to trust that Sidney knew what he was doing. That was his whole point in getting in touch with him again.

At the end of the e-mail was a link to a webpage for registration. Carl followed the link and was surprised to find that the form was somewhat lengthy, not only asking for standard contact information, but also requesting detailed information about his practice. What kind of practice? Years in existence? Gross revenues for the last three years? Collections for the last three years? New patients for the last two years? Number of staff and staff configuration? Percentage of what kinds of insurance? Overhead percentage? And a check off list for IT and equipment. The form also asked about 'competition' – group practices in their area. Which ones and how many offices within a 25-mile radius.

After looking over the form, Carl realized Sidney had been serious about the homework he'd have to do for the workshop. With all his other practice duties, it took Carl three days to get all the information onto the form. After putting the numbers together, Carl was getting a clearer view of his practice and its performance over the last few years. He also discovered that there were three groups in his area, not only Smile Right Now and Stratford, but also another large entity, Atlantic Dental, had just opened two new offices in Madison. He had shared this discovery with Veronica one night and she had quipped, "Invasion of the practice snatchers!" Carl had laughed at the time, but recognized that the group phenomenon could be knocking on his door next, coming for him.

Once Carl was sure he had all the information accurately complete, he submitted it. In a moment an alert appeared on his screen:

> *Welcome to the Managed Group Practice workshop. After we have received and processed your registration, you will be contacted by our office to review this information and outline your pre-workshop homework assignment.*

Carl stared at the words "managed group practice." He wasn't sure what that meant. He wasn't sure what managed group practice had to do with him and his situation. Maybe he'd registered for the wrong thing. He figured he'd wait until he got the call. He was also concerned about the pre-workshop homework. He thought the long online form was his homework. *Man, he thought, Sidney is piling it on. What have I gotten myself into?*

Carl didn't have to wait long to find out. The following morning he had an email waiting with options for a one hour call to review his registration and provide him with the assignment. Carl selected 8:00 PM that night. He badly wanted to know what he was signing up for.

Carl took the call that night in his study as he was reviewing the information he had sent in.

"Hello, Dr. Oldquist?"

"Yes, this is Carl."

"Hello, Dr. Oldquist, my name is Dr. Sergio Martinez. I am a mentor for Dr. Kaprov. I'll be going over your materials, asking a few questions, and reviewing your homework assignment. Is this a good time to talk?"

"Sure. And please call me Carl."

"Great. And I go by Sergio. Do you have any questions before we get started?"

"Yes, Sergio. What is *managed group practice*? And how'd you get to be a mentor in it?"

"Good questions, Carl. Let me start with how I got to be a mentor. Dr. Kaprov recognized that dentists need support and coaching. He recruited a few graduates of his recent programs to become mentors, just like Kois and Spears do in their work. There are now seven mentors in Sidney's formal mentor program."

"How many dentists have been through this workshop?" Carl asked.

"About 120 in the last two years. Dental practice is undergoing major change and dentists need someone who understands these changes and can address them."

"This managed group practice thing is a surprise for me. I thought the workshop would be more like a typical CE program with coaching to improve my practice situation," Carl shared.

"This workshop is much more than CE discourse. You'll be learning about deep structural changes occurring throughout the industry and the impact these changes are having on dental practice. You'll discuss the many possible pathways you can take to maximize your clinical skills and your existing assets. You'll learn about the different types of managed group practices that are in existence. And, most important, you'll begin the process of figuring out what path best suits your own situation."

"That's what's got me a bit troubled, Sergio. This managed group practice approach isn't at all what I expected. When I worked with Sidney five years ago, it was about solo private practice and how to make it great. Now it seems to be about group practice, and I'm not sure what that has to do with me."

"I understand, Carl. I get the same response from most dentists. Here's the bottom line as Sidney sees it: by the end of the decade over 80 percent of dentists practicing in this county will be in group practices of some sort or another." Sergio paused. "And by then solo practices will be worthless because no one will be buying solo practices."

It took Carl a moment to process the magnitude of the numbers. "And Sidney really believes the days of solo practices are numbered?"

"For the most part, yes. I know it's tough to swallow, but in Taos he'll show you all the data that supports his assertions about group and solo practices. Sidney wants dentists to get ahead of this curve and make decisions that are going to secure a solid future for them. He sees what's happening in the industry. He feels certain that solo practice has a short shelf life.

"This won't surprise you, Carl, but most practices have been flat for a while now. Did you know that patient expenditures in dental offices are down and continue to decline? And the number of patient visits per office is trending downward. The curve is headed downhill for solo practice."

"Well," Carl admitted, "I guess I thought it was just me."

"No, it's endemic. Currently, seven out of ten patients seen in dental offices nationwide have some form of dental plan, and that's going to increase. According to the information you submitted, 60% to

70% of your practice is third party reimbursement. And it's just going to get tougher. Although they haven't done it yet, insurance companies are going to keep on squeezing, and I mean squeezing real hard on fees. And I know you're very aware that practice expenses are going up and up. It's pretty obvious that solo practice can't sustain itself in these conditions."

"Why is it happening now?"

"It's complex and you'll hear the underlying reasons at the workshop, but I don't want to imply that it's all doom and gloom. Sidney views the changes in our industry as a tremendous opportunity. And that's what we hope you'll come to understand in Taos. I've followed Sidney's advice with my own practice, and I've never been happier or more satisfied than I am now. Ever."

Carl perked up. He needed that sense of hope, of possibility. "So, what's my next step? What should I do to prepare for the workshop?"

"Well, your official pre-workshop assignment is to read the book *How the Mighty Fall* by Jim Collins. But let's go over the numbers you submitted to make sure I understand the condition of your practice."

Over the next 45 minutes, Sergio grilled him on his numbers, the staff, the kind of patients he was getting, his current marketing, the top twenty procedures he did in his office, and insurance plans.

"Solid information, Carl. This will really help us provide answers when we're in Taos."

"I'm going to need that help, I guess."

"Everyone does, but like I said, this isn't about the end of the road, it's about bridging to a better future."

CHAPTER 6

The days leading up to the workshop in Taos had been chaotic. Between juggling the work schedule and family commitments, Carl hadn't had a chance to finish the book assignment. He figured he could power through it on the plane, though an airplane seat wasn't the easiest place for him to concentrate.

Veronica dropped him off at the airport two hours early. After making it through the maze of TSA security and finding his gate, he was greeted with some mixed news. His flight to Dallas was delayed by an hour. On the one hand, being delayed was a pain; on the other hand, he'd have more time to finish reading the book.

He settled into a quiet area of an adjacent gate and opened his laptop bag to extract his iPad. He found a nice surprise. In typical Veronica style, she had left him a box of black licorice – his favorite! He opened the attached note:

> C,
> *Good luck! You always have me back home rooting for you. I love you.*
> V

Despite all the turmoil that threatened to drag their practice down, he was buoyed by Veronica's steadfast faith in him. More than ever, it made Carl want this trip to Taos to be successful. To show him the path forward. And he knew that meant he had to be prepared.

He powered up his iPad and dove back into *How the Mighty Fall.* He'd read other Collins books— *Good to Great, Great by Choice, Built to Last*—and was familiar with his style, so with his added determination he flew through the rest of the book before he boarded. On the plane he was able to go back through the entire book and make some notes.

Carl felt that Collins' bottom line in the book was those companies that sustained themselves through the great recession had stuck to their core values. They weren't smug, over confident, or prideful. They stayed in touch with reality. They didn't overestimate their competence or accomplishments. They realized that what they achieved in the past and their position in the markets had little to do with their viability in the future. That really resonated with Carl. He had worked hard and achieved a lot in his practice, but that did not guarantee future success—which was all too evident to him now.

Collins also surmised that many companies that failed in the recession of 2008 went out of existence because of excessive pride. That idea made Carl think about a recent study club meeting in which a very well-known dental consultant had dismissed large corporate group practices. The consultant had confidently predicted, "Solo practice would always be around. Nothing can top them. We're not medicine. These corporate practices have their place, but they won't affect you." That struck Carl as hubris — especially after listening to Sidney and reading Collins' book.

And Carl figured that these corporate franchises were now affecting him. It had to be one of the reasons his new patient numbers were dropping. The book helped him understand how solo practice might be headed for the cliff. To Collins, the companies that stuck to their core values and made tough decisions about evolving to meet the changing conditions, faced the brutal realities and their choices steered them clear of disaster.

Carl wondered if he was open to changing the way he thought about his practice. Changing the way he thought about being a dentist. Changing his views on group practice. Changing his entire future. As his plane descended into DFW, he wondered if he was built to handle that kind of change.

He snugged his seatbelt extra tight, hoping for a soft landing.

CHAPTER 7

After deplaning, Carl checked a monitor to confirm he was going to make his connection. It was on time and he had half an hour before boarding started. He began making his way to Terminal C around the curved hallway of Terminal A. As he walked past the Salt Lick Bar-B-Que, he heard someone call his name.

He turned to see a woman standing up. "Carl. Hey, Carl," she said. "What brings you to Dallas?"

Carl did a double take before recognizing Kathy Germain, a long-time dental colleague who owned a practice in Milwaukee, about 80 miles from Madison. They'd met in the Kois program early on in their careers and developed a camaraderie which they easily re-established when attending dental meetings, conventions and clinical workshops through the years. However, he hadn't seen her for a while and was glad to see a friendly face now.

"How are you, Kathy?" He gave her short, roundish frame a quick hug and she invited him to sit.

"Do you have time or are you catching another flight?" she asked.

"Sure, I've got some time before my flight to Santa Fe."

"Santa Fe?" Kathy asked, eyebrows raised.

"Yeah. I'm going there for a workshop. Actually, it's in Taos."

"Taos? Seriously? Are your going to Sidney Kaprov's ranch?"

Carl's eyes widened. "Yes. The Managed Group Practice workshop?"

"Bingo," Kathy said. "Sounds like you may be searching for some answers like I am?"

"Maybe," Carl said as he sat down. "Well, catch me up. What's going on with you and your practice?"

Over the next 15 minutes Kathy filled him in. Hearing Kathy's story of the downward slide of her practice was doubly troubling to Carl. Not only because it was so very similar to his own, but because Kathy was a dynamic clinician. She had boundless energy and enthusiasm and ran a tight ship with a committed staff. Sergio's warning was reaffirmed: if this downturn was affecting solo dentists like Kathy and himself, it must be happening to a whole lot of very good solo dentists.

Carl explained his own situation, his earlier trip to the ranch, and marveled at how similar their experiences were. As they walked to their gate, they caught up on each of their families. After boarding, they were able to persuade a business traveler to trade seats so they could talk more about the workshop as well as share their thoughts on the reading assignment.

Seemingly, in no time, they were landing in Santa Fe. As they exited the plane, Kathy asked one final question. "So, you've worked with Sidney before. I know he has a stellar reputation. But," she hesitated, "he's always been an advocate of solo practice. Do you think he's sold out to some big industry interest? Could he be on some corporate dental payroll?"

There was no hesitation in Carl's reply. "If I thought that for a moment, I wouldn't be here. I may have my doubts about the course of action I'm going to need to take to save my practice, but I have no doubt that whatever Sidney is teaching is what *he* believes to his core. He'd never lower himself to shill for something he didn't believe in."

"That's good to hear because this is serious business we're getting ourselves into," Kathy said flatly.

"That's the truth," Carl acknowledged, feeling a sudden thrill of anticipation run down his spine, knowing he'd be on his way to the ranch soon. He wondered to himself if Fierce Eagle, Richard, would be here to pick them up—and if he'd remember Carl, aka Failing Mouse.

CHAPTER 8

Richard looked almost exactly as Carl remembered him: tall, long braided hair with a touch more gray, a dark denim blue work shirt, faded jeans and Jensen boots. Carl approached him.

"Hello, Richard," he said extending his hand, "I'm Carl Oldquist. You might remember me from a few years back when I came to Taos. It's good to see you."

"Good to see you, too, Carl. I do remember you and hope things have been well."

"Not too bad, though business could be better which is the reason I'm back. Richard, this is Dr. Kathy Germain."

Richard turned toward Kathy and said, "Pleased to meet you, Dr. Germain. I'm Sidney's ranch manager. The other workshop participants are at the ranch. Looks like you've just got your carry-ons; let me bring the van around. I'll be back in five minutes."

"Didn't you bring your old Ford 150?" Carl tried to kid, remembering his previous trip in that well-worn truck.

"No, with the three of us, it would've been a squeeze," Richard said with the slightest of grins. He turned and strode off.

Carl and Kathy walked out of the pueblo style terminal building to the arrival lanes where they stood by the curb. The temperature was crisp and the sky was clear. Carl recalled his earlier visit in his bones, as much as his memory.

"Seems like a nice fellow," Kathy observed.

"He's more talkative than the last time I was here; he's a man of few words, I tell you. But when Richard does say something, I've learned it's wise to listen. Very perceptive. And his wife, Dawn, is a fantastic cook. So get set for some good down-home southwestern meals."

"Sounds wonderful," Kathy said as Richard pulled up in an all-white van. He helped them with their luggage and they were quickly on their way. Richard, as usual, didn't mess around.

As they pulled onto the interstate Kathy asked, "How far is the ranch?"

"About 70 miles north, mostly highway. Should take us about an hour and half this time of evening," said Richard.

Over the first part of the trip, Kathy tried to engage Richard with questions like 'How many horses and ranch hands on the property?' He always responded politely and matter-of-factly, but did not elaborate.

Gradually, they slipped into quiet repose which was fine with Carl. He was enjoying the vast open countryside in the gathering dusk. So different than Madison. The majestic Sangre de Cristo mountains, the endless stretches of wire and wood fences, the sweeping stands of black pine trees, autumn sage, bear grass and buffalo juniper. The mesmerizing landscape made him realize how large and varied America was and how many possibilities and opportunities it contained. It was literally a land of change—and change didn't have to be onerous or frightening.

The passing scenery helped settle Carl, though when Richard finally turned off onto a side road and came to the wooden arch carved deeply with the words, 'Values Ranch and Retreat Center,' he felt his stomach tighten a bit. A hint of both anticipation and nervousness. Like last time, this was a big step he was taking.

After entering through the main gate, they pulled up to a roundabout in front of the massive rounded twelve foot tall oak doors of the main house—just as Carl remembered them—but Richard continued on down the drive another thirty yards and stopped in front of a building that wasn't there last time. It was a two story adobe structure fashioned in the same architecture as the main house. The entrance was one single large door, with the same heavy oak as the main house, but rectangular and only about eight feet high. More change.

As Richard was retrieving their luggage, the door opened. Sidney and a woman emerged into the porch light. Sidney was in full western regalia with his cowboy boots, pearl button denim shirt, his two inch leather belt with large metal buckle with the word VALUOCITY engraved on it, and an open denim coat with sheepskin lining. He was ranch ready. He flashed Carl and Kathy a big smile.

"Welcome to Taos! Glad you're here, Carl, and you too, Kathy. This is Sonia," he said as he motioned to Richard's slender sister-in-law. "Like Richard, she makes sure that everything on the ranch runs smoothly. Let's get you folks out of this chill and into the house."

He genteelly ushered them inside the spacious foyer. "Hope your flights were uneventful. I know you've had a long day, so I don't want to chitchat too much. We'll have plenty of time for that at breakfast. Dawn made welcome baskets for each of you so you can have a snack and unwind. Carl, there's a couple beers in your fridge, because I remember you have a fondness for microbrews. Any questions before I let Sonia show you to your rooms?"

"Too many questions, Sidney," Carl said, "but those can wait until tomorrow because we're hoping you'll have answers."

Sidney clapped Carl on the shoulder and laughed. "Well, you know I'm not so much about absolutes and answers as I am about opportunities and possibilities. I've been listening to a lot of Dylan these days and he had it right, 'The times they are a' changing.' The purpose of this workshop is to get you ahead of the change. So, sleep well. We'll see you at 8:00 AM for one of Dawn's signature ranch breakfasts."

They said their goodbyes. Carl thanked Richard for the ride and Richard tipped his hat to Carl. When he got to his room, Carl realized how drained he felt, but he found some of Dawn's homemade cornbread in his basket, still warm, and took a bite. Immediately revived, he went to the fridge, pulled out and opened a Taos Mesa Amarillo Rojo beer. Then he called Veronica.

"Made it, honey. The black licorice was a nice surprise, as was your note. Why are you so good to me?"

"Must be habit."

"Well, that's one habit I hope doesn't change because Sidney is hinting that change is our new constant."

"I guess I'll have to mix it up then. Next time it'll be red licorice."

They chatted about the day's travel and the surprise of meeting up with Kathy, whom Veronica had met at a state dental meeting a couple years back. When Carl finally crawled into bed, he felt a great comfort from across the many miles he'd traveled. The large window revealed a harvest moon just over the horizon, but Carl was asleep before he had much time to marvel.

CHAPTER 9

Carl woke at 6:25 AM, five minutes before his alarm. He'd slept soundly in the cool air, under a lush Navajo patterned wool blanket. He showered and dressed in jeans and a flannel shirt, then made a cup of coffee in the Keurig on the desk in the room. He drank his coffee looking out the window to the deep blue mountain sky. He felt rested and ready.

A little before 8:00, he headed to the main house where the dining area was located just off the Great Room. Kathy and another gentleman were already seated in well worn leather chairs by the main fireplace.

"Good morning. Sleep well?" Kathy asked and Carl nodded. "There's another doc in the dining room already, but we were being chatty. Carl, this is Dr. Vincent Delfino."

"Please call me Vinny," he said as he rose to shake Carl's hand.

"Vinny's from Philadelphia. He has a practice in Chestnut Hill. His dad was a dentist before him and it was his dad's practice until he retired nine years ago. Did I get that right, Vinny?"

"Absolutely."

Carl thought Vinny looked like Dean Martin with graying hair. "Please to meet you, Vinny. I'm sure we're all going to learn a lot about our practices, though I'm betting we're all pretty much in the same boat."

Vinny gave a grim smile. "That's what Kathy and I were just talking about. Up until two years ago my practice was growing at a steady, reliable pace. When my dad left the practice, I bought a 5,200 square foot stone and brick home built in the early 1900s. A beauty—oak floors, lots of original interior work. I converted it into a five operatory dental office with a small lab, staff lounge, private offices, totally wired."

Carl smiled at Vinny's heavy Philly accent.

"Like Kathy, things were going pretty good until 2008. Had two full time hygienists, three at the front desk, a full time associate who was wonderful, and four assistants. I was grossing about two million a year. No worries about new patients. Hygiene was almost too full. No complaints."

Vinny paused and met Carl's eyes. "And then, like probably all of us here, I'm guessing, it started to slide. Slow, not fast."

"Yeah, it's been a roller coaster," Carl commiserated, "though a lot more down than up."

Sonia approached and apologized for interrupting. She handed each of the three a name tag and invited them to the dining room, "If you'll take your seats now, Sidney is ready to get started with breakfast and introductions."

The dining room was spacious with floor-to-ceiling windows looking out towards the mountains and a rising sun. At the heavy planked knotty pine table were six settings. Sidney sat at one end and motioned them to the empty chairs. Carl took a seat next to a handsome gentleman with a dark complexion. Carl glanced at the man's tag and saw his name with the designation 'Mentor' printed in red underneath it: Dr. Sergio Martinez.

"Hi, Sergio, I'm Carl. We spoke on the phone. Good to meet you in person."

"You too, Carl," Sergio said shaking his hand vigorously.

With everyone seated, Sidney started the proceedings. "Good morning and welcome to Taos. Dawn and Sonia will be serving us breakfast in a moment. I'd like to use this time to get to know each other. Anyone need coffee before we start?"

Carl raised his hand, 'Black, please."

"First, I want you to be reassured that even though we'll talk a lot about change over the next two days, some things will always remain. I'm hoping that one of these things is a sense of camaraderie and purpose that you as a group will build. So, with that in mind, I'm going to ask each of you to take a minute or so and let us know who you are, where you come from, and a little about your practice."

Sidney turned to Carl. "Carl, since you've been to the ranch before I'll ask you to go first."

The sudden attention flustered Carl for a moment. He didn't want to be looked on as special for having been to Taos before, but he did appreciate that Sidney had recognized him in a small way. "Should I stand up?" he asked hesitantly.

"Heavens, no," Sidney chuckled as he reached for a piece of cornbread in one of the baskets near him. "This is very informal. Try to think of this as a family meal. We'll all be eating as we share."

"In that case," Carl reached for a piece of cornbread himself and relaxed, "I'm Carl Oldquist from Madison, Wisconsin. I have an amazing wife who sometimes has to bail me out in the office, a son in his first year of college and a daughter who can now drive. I've been in practice for 22 years and things have never been better or worse business-wise than in the past five."

He took a small bite of the cornbread. "Man, this is good. Dawn is a fantastic cook. I'm lucky to have tasted it before when I was out here. The reason I came five years ago was because my practice almost tanked. Following Sidney's core values approach, my wife and I got the practice back on track and did well, but recently it's been struggling again and it's not for the same reasons. I'm here to learn what those reasons are and I how I can be successful again."

Carl looked around the table and everyone was nodding their head. He had a sense that not only had they understood where his practice was, each of them were living some variation of the same story.

Sidney chimed in. "Thanks, Carl. I think we all understand where you're coming from. Kathy why don't you go next, then we'll have Steve and Vinny follow."

Over the course of a hearty breakfast, Carl got a better sense of the other two dentists gathered there. They were certainly birds of a feather hit by a perfect storm of circumstances beyond their control. Like him, they were all struggling and he knew that in rooting for them to succeed, he was rooting for himself. Silently, he suspected that was one of the reasons Sidney had started the morning this way. Create a sense of community and shared purpose. All for one and one for all.

CHAPTER 10

Sergio was the last one at the table to introduce himself, at Sidney's request.

"Hi, I'm Sergio Martinez. I'm married with three children, ages 12, 10 and 5. All boys, all trouble, all the time." A few at the table chuckled.

"I've been in practice 16 years. We now have three locations in Texas: Houston, Galveston and Beaumont. We have three associates who are employees; one will become a junior partner later this year. We have two specialists, a periodontist and an endodontist that work in all three locations a day or two a week depending on schedules. We have a solid executive team, seven assistants, nine hygienists and six front desk staff. We have a small satellite office for business and finance functions; payables, receivables, and ordering supplies. We just hired a COO and one of our office managers is being promoted this week to regional manager. We have it configured this way because our five year strategy is to develop a managed group practice with about 12 to 15 offices."

Questions popped up rapidly in Carl's mind as Sergio spoke. *Why do you need a COO? How can a guy this young be so successful? What does this have to do with me and my situation?*

Sergio wrapped up his introduction. "The practice has been growing at a solid 19%, some locations a little stronger than others. Last year we did a little over five and half million. And I am looking at acquiring two more practices this year and to reach ten million within a year and half after acquisition. I owe a lot of my success to Sidney and his coaching, and that's why I'm here. To help other dentists achieve the success I have."

To Carl, it was like hearing a dentist from another planet: multiple practices, COO, associates, 20 plus staff, ten million dollars. It felt alien to someone in Carl's position.

Sidney spoke up. "I want to point out a few things before we go on. There are many different kinds of managed group practices which will be part of our discussion later. I want to point out that Sergio used the pronoun 'we' rather than 'I' in describing his situation. That was very intentional and another critical element we'll get to this afternoon."

As Sergio finished introducing himself, Carl had a sudden feeling that he was in the wrong place, at the wrong workshop, in an entirely different world of dentistry. But Sidney didn't give him time to dwell on the shock by quickly taking the reins.

"I wanted Sergio here so you could begin to see where you fit in, where the future lies for you. As I've said, in my estimation the future is group practice. You're here to learn about group practice and then determine if it's for you." He paused and after assessing the silence, asked, "That may feel like a bombshell, so tell me what's going through your mind right now."

Kathy spoke right up. "I'm a bit overwhelmed and having real trouble following this conversation. Quite honestly, I'm not sure what a managed group practice is."

"I doubt you're alone, Kathy," Sidney acknowledged. "As I said, there are many different models of managed group practice. There are group practices that are internally managed, like Sergio's, and some that are externally managed by a Managed Service Organization (MSO). There are small, locally managed group practices and there are very large, well-established national groups. Then there are many more that are in-between. Most managed group practices are experiencing strong growth and rapid expansion and many are attracting significant capital investment."

"Okay, so how do dentists like us fit into this spectrum of group practices?" Kathy followed up, glancing around the table.

When Sidney answered he was looking directly at Kathy, yet speaking to everyone in the room. "Over the last few decades, dentists have made the leap from being well-trained technicians treating dental disease and improving esthetics to being competent individual owners, leaders and managers, able to run solo or very small partnered practices as highly successful businesses.

"But managed group practice is taking center stage for many reasons. And the number of solo practices is declining at a rapid rate. In 2008, 76 percent of the practices in the U.S. were solo. By 2010 it was down to 69 percent. If you follow the trend, that means by 2020 solo practice may represent a minority of all practices in the U.S.

"So, the question to ask yourself, and I know how hard this is, but you are here today because you understand at some level that the question needs to be answered: Can you survive as a solo practice in this changing ecology of dental practice? Can you compete with group practices? Can you distinguish yourself enough to stay profitable for years to come? Or, in order to remain viable, is your best chance with a managed group practice?"

Carl didn't even know how to begin to answer that challenge, but Steve Busman, the dentist sitting directly across from him spoke up. "With all due respect, Sidney, as I told everyone when I introduced myself, I've been in solo practice 24 years. I don't want to change. I just want my practice to be good enough to pay the bills now and fund my retirement in ten years or so. I'm leery about being in a group practice. I don't want to lose control or my independence. Is this 'group' thing really our only choice? It seems like such a drastic solution to the changes in the industry."

"Change doesn't ask permission," Sidney answered calmly. "Look. I understand how personal this is for all of you, but my role here is to show you what's happening in dentistry and help you take on the changes as an owner, the one person who has to make the tough decisions. If you as owner don't make tough, intentional decisions, then the market will make them for you."

He looked directly at Steve. "Steve, you say you're worried you'll lose control if you join a group practice, but the truth is you've already lost control. The context, the conditions for dentistry in our nation have changed. You can't keep doing things the same way. You've recognized this and that's why you're here today. Remember, as an owner your job is to increase the negotiable value of your asset, the practice, every year. By every measure your solo practice is decreasing in value."

"How do you know that?" Steve asked, challenging Sidney.

"Simple math. The pool of individual buyers for practices is drying up. Dental students and residents have $300,000 - $400,000 in debt when they get out of school. If you add in the sale of the average practice, which at its height might have been around $1.2 million, that means a recent graduate would be paying anywhere between $8,000 and $10,000 a month if they bought a practice. That's getting tougher and tougher for new dentists to afford. And, without a buyer, an asset turns into a liability. That's one of the new realities in our industry that I'm trying to get all of you to see."

The only sound around the table came from the fire crackling out in the Great Room.

CHAPTER 11

Sidney broke the heavy silence at the table. "You know, Steve, early on, when I attempted to explain the future of dentistry as 'group practice' by going from the past forward, in essence predicting the future, I could see I wasn't getting through to my audience. They resisted the idea. They were too attached to the past and couldn't accept anything different in their futures.

"So I tried a different tack. I put myself in the shoes of a Social Archaeologist, in effect looking back at the model of solo practice. Imagine someone 20, maybe 30 years in the future, spreading out the bones of a solo practice on his examination table, dissecting it, determining how and why it ultimately became extinct."

There was expectancy growing at the table. Sidney could see it in their faces. And it always happened when he set the stage this way.

"Is there such a thing as a social archaeologist?" Steve asked.

"Yes. This type of archaeologist focuses on the big picture rather than the individual picture, and tries to build a model of a group of people and ascertain why their civilization and/or culture thrived or failed. So, I took that approach with dentistry, particularly solo dental practice.

"Like any archaeologist with an artifact he or she is trying to decipher, I imagine myself sitting at a large table with pieces of an ancient solo practice in front of me. I see a single dentist running a small business, managing a staff of seven, responsible for a majority of the revenue of the practice, wearing all the hats (leadership, ownership, management, marketing), and taking all the risk. When I look at the layers of history that predated this dentist and his practice, I can see that for decades this particular model worked well. And then the climate of dental practice changed in the early 2000's and revenue and doctor compensation flattened out. The statistics actually show that income began to flatten *before* the recession. Then in 2008, things really went poorly for dental practice owners; especially the solo dentists.

"This particular solo practice I have on my table continued to struggle and decline while new models of dental care delivery emerged and prospered. These new models were the early attempts at group dental practice. The new model was resisted, it was criticized and purported to be an affront to the dentist-patient relationship. It was deemed cancerous to the industry and to the health of dental patients.

"As a Social Archaeologist I see the relic on my table. As well I can watch history march on and see solo practices failing and closing while groups are learning new and better ways to deliver dentistry and improve patient health, both dental and physical. These early group practices learned how to scale and see a wider range of patient while increasing their profit and efficiencies. The underserved were being seen at a greater rate. The overall health of citizens was improved at a lower cost. Big data emerged and dental groups learned how to better serve each patient in ways that a solo doctor simply could not. They had the resources of a group behind them in delivering the best care possible.

"And these groups mingled and learned at an accelerated rate. They merged and fulfilled their visions as solo dentists were never intended to do. As multicellular organisms they completely reinvented dental health care. Technology evolved dramatically and groups could afford and take advantage of these new tools.

"Solo dentists were the seeds of dentistry. They grew tall and healthy, until they were established in the earth. They created the foundation and then the bridge to a better way. Solo dentists were important in their day. But a time came when they simply couldn't bear the weight of a single practice any longer. This practice in front of me died. It closed, unable to keep up and deliver care in the new ecology."

After a few moments while the group digested his explanation, Sidney asked, "Does that make sense?"

Steve chimed in first. "Too much sense when you put it that way. I still don't like what's happening and I'm not wild about leaping into a group practice, but I'm beginning to understand the context better, Sidney."

"And context is decisive, as I've always said," Sidney reminded them.

Every one chuckled. They all knew that about Sidney. He looked at his watch. "I understand you might need a little time to process some of these ideas, so let's take a thirty minute break and then reconvene here. I advise taking a stroll outside and enjoying the freshest air anywhere. It might help clear some of the consternation I may have just created. See you in half an hour."

Kathy grabbed Carl's arm by the sleeve with a glazed look in her eyes. "Let's get some of that fresh air, Carl. I need to clear the cobwebs after Sidney's bombshell."

"I'm all for that," Carl said, hoping he didn't look as shell-shocked as he felt.

CHAPTER 12

Kathy and Carl walked out the main entrance and towards a cluster of large ponderosa pines near the main house. The sun had grown bright in the cloudless sky and the chill of the night had disappeared, but it was still cool enough that Kathy wrapped an Alpaca wool shawl around her shoulders.

Carl drew in a deep breath. "It's an awful lot to digest all at once."

Kathy nodded. "That's for sure."

"It's like waking up in a foreign country and not knowing the language or the culture," Carl continued.

"I agree, though, at the same time I can see the similarities in my own situation and the other docs here, even the one in the managed group practice," Kathy acknowledged. "I'm thinking if he can figure this out, I can, too."

"Well, that's encouraging, though I'm not sure it's for me," Carl admitted, looking back towards the main house, noticing an approaching figure.

It was Sergio. "Mind if I join you?"

"Not at all," Kathy said with a smile. "I think there's enough mountain air for everyone."

Sergio smiled back. "I love the setting here. So, what are your thoughts about what you heard at breakfast?"

"It's…a lot," Kathy answered. "A lot to take in."

Carl agreed. "Both Kathy and I have been in solo practice all our professional lives. I have over twenty years experience owning my own shop, being the boss. I have zero experience working in groups, although I have been on some committees for our state association." He paused. "And the truth is I hated it. But that's my only experience working with other dentists."

Sergio looked from Carl to Kathy. "When I came to Taos to learn about group practice three years ago I was just where you are now. I had a serious lack of understanding and knowledge about managed groups. I'd had that same experience working with other dentists, Carl, but we didn't have anything at-stake financially, so issues usually fell flat or seemed to drift away without any resolution. I could be friends with most of the dentists, but I wouldn't have considered being in business with them."

"So what changed your mind?" Carl asked.

Sergio motioned to the tall ponderosa pines around them. "During a break when I was here three years ago, I was asking Sidney the same kind of questions you're asking now. And in typical Sidney fashion he didn't answer my question. He asked one. He said, 'Why has this stand of trees survived? Why do you rarely see a solitary tree in this whole landscape?

"Sidney used this stand of trees right here to help me see that in nature groups survive and thrive. They protect each other and use resources more efficiently. A solitary tree is more vulnerable to storms and disease, to changing conditions, while a stand of trees can weather tempests better by providing buffers and interlocking root systems. Strength in numbers. Sidney showed me how this connected to the new dental landscape.

"Once I understood what was going on in our industry as a whole," Sergio expounded, "I saw that group practice is a fait accompli. That prompted me to get together with a few dentists in my area. People I could trust, people I admired, dentists I've known a long time. We explored the possibility of putting a group together. We chose who we wanted to work with. We set up the parameters of a new practice. We built it according to our shared values. At the end, we pulled the trigger because it just made a lot of sense. And as I said at breakfast, we're over two years into it and we're now hiring real executives. We are also entertaining the idea of equity partners."

"How hard was it?" Kathy asked.

Sergio smiled. "Well, lots of work. Meetings, phone calls, site visits to other managed groups, talking to lawyers. But the hardest part was learning to operate as a group, not as a cluster of individuals."

"Why do you think that is?" Kathy probed further.

"Because dentists think *I* not *we*. *My* practice. *My* staff. They do this for many reasons: the culture of dental school where it was everyone for themselves;

the consultants and dental practice magazines with a dentist on the cover, typically someone who has built their professional Taj Mahal, claiming to work three and a half days a week making $2 million; the personality of dentists; and, of course, fear."

"Fear?" Carl interjected.

"Fear of not looking good. Fear of loss of control. Fear of trusting others. Fear of taking a risk. Like many medical practitioners, dentists are mostly risk averse. That's why they went into dentistry in the first place. It was seemingly a guaranteed way to make a good living for life. Open a practice, get patients, make good money, everyone needs a dentist." Sergio paused. "I think we thought it would go on forever, but, as Sidney is trying to point out, those days of hanging a shingle and having it just work out are long gone."

Sergio looked to the west, towards the sweeping horizon. "Sidney suggested I speak to you because he knows you and thinks that possibly you two might consider forming your own group. In terms of population, demographics, core values and service mix, it seems to be a fairly ideal situation for a regional managed group."

Kathy glanced at Carl. He saw that her searching gaze was questioning but also full of possibility. Could they put their own group together? Could they do what Sergio had done? Sergio was right there telling them it could be done—and he had done it!

For a moment the dread and uncertainty Carl had been battling gave way to a sense of excitement, of possibility, of challenge. "That," Carl said wrinkling his brow, "is an intriguing idea, Sergio." He locked eyes with Kathy. "But, I'm going to have to know a lot more about this first."

"Agreed," Kathy chimed back.

As they walked back to the house, Carl felt oddly invigorated. Yes, the break and the fresh air had helped, but it was more that there was a clearer, more concrete vision of a future that wasn't being dealt them by default, but by the possibility of choice and creation.

CHAPTER 13

When they reconvened at the large pine table in the dining room, it had been cleared of Dawn's sumptuous breakfast, but there was an addition. A large high definition screen was sitting at the end of the table showing a middle-aged man sitting on a stool.

Sidney directed their attention to the monitor. "Hope you had a chance to absorb some of the information from our breakfast session. There are a couple folks I'd like you to hear from, so we've Skyped them. I'd like to welcome Dr. Thomas Deville. He's the CEO of a group in Pennsylvania with 23 practices. I invited him to tell a bit about his journey into managed group practice. Tom, would you please introduce yourself to our group."

The man on the screen waved. "Hello. As Sidney said I'm Tom Deville. I really appreciate the opportunity to share my experience because not too long ago I was in your shoes. I'd been a solo practitioner for 18 years with a solid practice. I kept up on things with CE and consulting. I was in study clubs, went to Canada to learn implants, did a ton of practice management courses, had big time consultants come and work with me and my staff, and had a practice management coach. The whole nine yards. I'm sure Sidney has pointed out to you that times have changed and dentistry has too. I believe that what you'll learn with Sidney can give you what you need to get started.

But, it's not a one-size-fits-all formula. You'll need to work out a lot for yourselves since every practice, every owner, every market is different.

"You might build a group practice. You might join an existing managed group. Or you might decide not to join a group practice at all and just stay the course. It is always your choice; it has to be because you need to be invested in the work to be successful. The idea is that when you leave Sidney's workshop, you'll be able to make the most well-informed choice possible—no matter what that choice is."

Steve spoke up and his voice had a bit of an edge to it. "No disrespect, Dr. Deville, but I worked with Sidney years ago and my practice boomed. Now I'm feeling a little betrayed with this whole group practice approach. Rather than figure out how to have solo practices be successful, you and Sidney and Sergio are telling us that corporate dentistry is the *only* way to go."

Sidney spoke up. "Steve, let me just say that I've heard this before: that I've somehow turned traitor. As I explained earlier at breakfast, we may not like the changes that are happening, but we shouldn't ignore them. Dentistry is changing and there is no stopping those larger economic forces. I, for one, chose not to ignore these changes and began looking at the best way forward for my clients. That's why we're here. That's why Sergio is here and Tom is Skyping with us.

"You know, Steve, when the wheat industry was working on modifying wheat to produce more kernels, they discovered that as more kernels were produced, the wheat stalk wasn't strong enough to stay upright, and leaned over. In the same way, the burden of solo practice is becoming increasingly difficult to sustain for a single dentist nowadays."

"It's still tough to reconcile, Sidney. It stings," Steve said with his mouth set tight.

"It should sting, Steve. It means you care about what you've poured your blood, sweat, and tears into for so many years. What makes it tougher still is that we have a vocal chorus of dental pundits, consultants, and professional associations feeding you the fairy tale that solo practice is invulnerable to these changing conditions. And it's easy to buy that line because it's what you want to hear. We're all susceptible to selective listening, but in a world that's changed as rapidly as ours, with the advent of the Internet and entire industries like newspapers, telecommunications, brick and mortar retail all having to reinvent themselves to survive, dentists can't stick their head in the sand and hold on tight to the belief that 'This too shall pass.' We've got to adapt, we've got to reinvent ourselves to survive. And for me, that reinvention is centered on managed group practice."

Sidney let that sink in for a few moments and then Vinny spoke up. "I think we all understand that things are changing in the industry—certainly my quarterly numbers tell that in an alarming way. So, what are we supposed to do about it? Like most dentists, I've invested myself, my time, my energy, into solo practice. I don't know anything about groups, how they work, how they operate and even whether I can join a group, or even how I'd find a group I'd want to join. I can't make a decision without looking at some of the nuts and bolts."

"Absolutely," Sidney responded. "The goal for today and tomorrow is to provide you with an overview of the costs and benefits of making a choice about group practice. Those costs and benefits will differ based on your situation. As Tom explained, some of you may decide to build group practices, some of you may join existing manage groups, and some of you will simply continue as a solo practice and circle the wagons."

"Circling the wagons doesn't sound like a very good option," Vinny said.

"Only if you think what's happening with your practices right now is a passing wave, a temporary condition," Sidney said. "I don't believe it is. I believe the cause is deep and structural and requires dentists to rethink how they do business. So the question is, are you ready to face it?"

The room was silent.

"Remember," Sidney said, "we're not here to tell you what choice to make. We hope to provide you with enough information to make the best possible choice—for you and your practice. If that seems fair, let's move on with what Tom has to share."

Steve nodded as did Vinny. Carl glanced over at Kathy who responded with a thumbs-up gesture. Carl did the same. He knew it was time to dig in and get started on what a group practice might mean for him.

CHAPTER 14

Tom continued. "I want to acknowledge that what Steve expressed is very common. This kind of change shakes you to your bones, but it can be revitalizing as well. So, let me continue with my story. A couple years into my practice, I got it into my head that I wanted to create something bigger professionally. I'd taken some business classes at Penn and I really enjoyed the 'creative' aspect of business. So, I purchased a couple practices in town and used my own systems with both. It went well, so I purchased a fourth practice in a small town about 25 miles away."

"How'd you pay for them?" asked Carl.

"My bank." Tom explained. "I was a young guy, but I had a banker who really had faith in my vision and he went to bat for me with the higher ups. A couple years flew by as I focused on the four practices and things were going pretty steady. We had good staff, great docs and were working like a well-oiled machine. It was then that I met a guy at an ADA meeting who had nine practices in southern Pennsylvania. He was more of a numbers guy, but we still had lots in common and similar ideas about the future. To make a long story short, we merged our 13 locations into a single entity and created a five-year plan to get us to 25-30 locations. We're four years into the strategic plan and we're currently ahead of target with 23 practices."

"You sure make it sound easy, Tom," Kathy remarked. "Is it that simple to find, purchase and finance practices?"

"No, it's not as simple as that. I kind of gave you the Cliffs Notes version. Finding the practices wasn't terribly hard. You hear things in a small town. But I was lucky enough to have a great office manager who was a huge help in getting my original four practices running efficiently. She handled the management side while I focused on the clinical. But with four locations I was starting to get a little burnt out, traveling back and forth to all four locations every week. When I ran into my eventual partner I was kind of up against it, not quite sure how to take the next step. But he, with his nine locations, had a COO and CFO type that were running and managing his operations. Then, when we merged, I gave up all those responsibilities. I can't tell you what a relief that was! I was able to focus on the clinical aspects of all the practices as the Chief Clinical Officer. And I really enjoyed that."

"So, you just gave up control of your four practices?" Steve chirped.

"Well, yes, and no. The big picture was a huge consideration as we talked about joining our practices. Listen, I've got one of our docs with me. He and his staff are here for a CE course. I thought it might be interesting to hear his side of the story. This is Matt Wilson."

A grey-haired man with receding hairline moved into the frame next to Tom. Matt waved. "Howdy to all of you. As you can probably see from my grey hair, or what's left of it, I'm a bit long in the tooth, and a few years back I was looking for a good exit strategy. I was 61 years old then and thinking I'd practice for five more years. I thought I could take the usual path, you know, sell, become a full time associate for a year or two, then a part time associate, then leave. You know, the way most dentists have done it for ages."

Carl nodded. He knew what Matt was talking about. The exit strategy of selling fifty percent of one's practice to a new dentist, partnering up for a couple years, then selling the other fifty percent with your associate-partner having right of first refusal. The so-called golden path.

"But I learned that practices in my area were selling for less than the year before, and less than the year before that. Clearly the values of solo practices were going downward. It might have been because there were fewer buyers available, what with student debt being so high and all. I'm not exactly sure. But for whatever reason, I had my practice on the market for a year and no one came close to matching what I thought it was worth.

"I was getting worried, so I started looking into other possibilities and began to think that being acquired by an established managed group practice might be a better option than finding a solo doc.

"That's how I eventually met up with Tom. Within a month of our meeting, Tom's group had appraised my practice and they valued it way higher than the broker I had hired. Incidentally, my broker told me that all he could get for my practice was about fifty percent of my previous year's gross. That didn't sit very well with me and I'm sure you'd feel the same way."

"Damn straight," Vinny interjected.

"Exactly," Matt said with a chuckle. "First, Tom and his group offered me a much better deal. More money for my practice, some cash right away and some in the form of stock, which gives me a tax break. Second, they were able to bring an associate into practice right away which kept things stable with staff. They also provided part time specialists rather than me having to refer out. And they wanted me to stay on and make sure my production stayed on top.

"After two years, going to their own CE programs, not having to manage the practice, having an associate and specialists on board, I was having the best time in practice I'd had in years. I didn't want to leave dentistry. They asked me to mentor some younger dentists in the area—which I loved doing. It's worked out great for me."

Vinny spoke up. "So, Matt, why do you think Tom paid more for your practice than a broker could muster?"

Matt looked at Tom who promptly answered. "That's a good question. In the open market, the asset value of stand-alone solo practices is rapidly decreasing. Recent graduates have no money. Banks are tight and getting tighter. A new dentist paying back a million dollar loan for a practice purchase on top of significant school debt is a minefield.

"On the other hand, the asset value of a practice when acquired by our group goes up over time because the stock value increases as we grow. We bought Matt's practice for 80% rather than the 50-60% the broker was working with. Matt was already ahead. Of that purchase price we gave him 80% cash and the rest in stock. This saves us from paying cash for every practice we purchase which makes for a stronger financial position, plus it defers money for Matt in the form of stock, which increases in value over time.

"As young dentists come on board, not only is our marketing and training top of the rank, these young dentists get busy and they get CE and eventually, they have the opportunity to buy into the business."

"So what does that mean to you if young dentists buy stock?" Vinny pressed.

Tom smiled. "If the company is well run, and we are very well run, practices all do better—and because we are acquiring more practices all the time, the stock value goes up. The stock I hold now is worth almost one and a half times more than when I first acquired it. So I am getting more money for my practice, far more, than if I'd sold it to some individual through a practice broker. In the final analysis, I'm going to end up getting close to a 110% of gross revenues—which is okay in my book."

"Works for me, too!" Vinny said with an emphatic slap of his hand on the table.

CHAPTER 15

The group laughed at Vinny's gesture. Sidney thanked Tom and Matt for sharing their experience and closed the Skype call. Then he stood up and walked over to a rolling white board.

"Okay," Sidney began, "we'll be covering a lot of ground in this next segment, but you don't need to take notes. We're recording our sessions and will send you the MP3 audio files by next Friday. So, feel free to ask questions as they come up for you.

"First, we're going to discuss the evolution of managed group practice to give you a little background. We've created a simple model which we hope will allow you to better understand the concepts. We call it *Acme Dental*. I think we came up with this name well into a second bottle of a nice California Syrah."

Kathy chuckled. "I'm a fan of wine-based brainstorming."

"As we all should be," Sidney agreed. "Just remember that there are many, many types of managed group practice, so keep in mind that Acme Dental is more illustrative than factual. It is not 'the' model, but we think it provides an easy to understand framework and structure of managed group practice.

"In our model there are four pretty basic steps for growth and development." Gesturing towards the white board, Sidney wrote the key words as he explained each step. "*Solo dentist*, that's you, sitting around this table. The second step is *Entrepreneur*. Commonly this stage is a single dentist with maybe 2-3 locations, but it can also be a partnership of two or three, who want to formalize and build a company. They have the itch, an entrepreneurial personality. They see a vision of themselves as building something better. They are willing to take risks and it's this willingness to take risks that separates them from other dentists."

Steve asked, "What if you don't see yourself as an entrepreneur?"

"Well, in that case, being acquired by a group may be your better choice. But for some, there is a dream to build something more substantial, not just a single practice," Sidney responded.

Steve wouldn't let go. "If the group practice model is so effective, why aren't there more group practices?"

"Dentists resist the group practice model for the same reason the Green Mountain Boys resisted the British—they like their independence. Dentists are smart, capable, self-driving professionals. Up until now they enjoyed successful careers managing their own practice. Does that make sense?"

Steve nodded and Sidney continued. "Now add decades of dentists practicing solo, and the belief that solo practice is the only answer is entrenched. Most dentists believe that group practice is a menace. Many professional associations are railing against what they term the 'corporate practice of dentistry.' Most consultants and pundits are reaffirming what they believe are the key principles of the dental profession; solo practice, fee-based compensation, individual dentist control over the services provided."

"Excuse me, Sidney," Sergio jumped in. "Often dentists can be resistant to group practice because it's not easy to get rid of the Lone Ranger mentality. They believe their individual smarts and superb technical skills will be stifled in a collaborative setting. Most dentists also believe that getting dentists to work together is a miserable task. I have found that couldn't be further from the truth."

"Thanks, Sergio," Sidney said returning to the white board. "Beyond *Entrepreneur* is *Leadership*. In moving to five or more locations, solid leadership is required. Whether it's the founding dentist or processional executives being brought in, there must be strong leadership to guide growth and build a solid culture. Then the *Grow and Replicate* phase, where you have a professionally managed business that is focused on acquiring or building new locations at a faster pace. Sergio will now start to take you deeper into each of these levels."

Sergio stood and started right in. "As a Solo practice you're the CEO, the COO, the CFO, HR and, well, everything. The buck stops with you. You do everything to grow your enterprise, but the bigger it becomes, no matter how good your systems, you have more to do. You can offload some responsibilities to staff members, but in the end, everything eventually runs through you. Right?

"At this level you have full control. But to sustain the kind of numbers you want, or need, you must be at the chair which means you have to do all the other stuff when you're not at the chair. So your days are long, very long. The practice can only grow to your own capacity to deliver. So, basically you carry all the weight of the practice on your shoulders. Remember Sidney's wheat metaphor?

"Most often your legal structure is not so critical. Typically, a solo practitioner relies on their accountant to dictate the legal structure which is solely dependent on minimizing tax consequences. Not for growth. Not for shared ownership. Not for being acquired or acquiring other practices. Nope, it's just about minimizing the tax liability.

"The next step is *Entrepreneur*. You have expressed your entrepreneurial inclinations and now have two, possibly three locations and one associate, maybe two associates. But you are still the engine—top producer, leader and manager—only now there is even more on your plate. Your hours are long, you get lots of interruptions throughout the day and stuff is dropping out because you can't be in two or three places at the same time. You probably can't make this leap without a really strong practice manager and an experienced staff. All locations are up and running, but your fingers are in everything, all the time. It has become overwhelming.

"At this level, one plus one does not equal two. It equals 'four' in terms of complexity. You have more staff issues; scheduling production becomes more complicated; scheduling assistants, hygiene checks, patient relations, and marketing all become more complex. But, you persevere, right? You add more structure, more systems and processes. And in time, things begin to run more smoothly. But you find that you still need to be the top producer and all the business issues continue to land on your desk.

"Often the solution is to simply add another associate, but to do that you need another location. So you might acquire a poor performing practice or an older dentist's practice and bring on another associate. However, you still find yourself working at the chair in several locations four days a week. You're probably wondering when the 'fun' starts. I know I was. Houston, Galveston and Beaumont are pretty good drives from each other."

Sergio looked around the table to make sure everyone was with him. "At this point you're working eighty hour weeks and you've got breakdowns galore. This is where most dentists get stuck, and retreat. Things are so hectic and stressful, your health and well-being may be at risk. You're in overdrive all the time. You may back off to one or two locations. Believe me it can be rough. When I was working three locations I felt like I was either chairside, in my car, or at my desk keeping up with all the operational demands. My wife was unhappy and my kids were always in bed by the time I got home. You've got to be prepared for some sacrifice to get to the next level.

"However, the good news is if you can make it to the next level, if you can stick with your vision, you have a real opportunity. A group will have been birthed."

Sergio pointed to the board. "The next stage is *Leadership*. This is not leadership by command and control, but leadership by vision and influence. This is when you must move into a real leadership role and begin to entrust others who have committed to the values, vision and mission of the practice. You realize you need to let go of making every decision and that is really, really hard. This is where you start building the essential foundation for a managed group to evolve."

Sidney stood. "And that's a great place to pause because a number of fundamental decisions need to be made at this point. Many of these decisions fall into the legal domain. But before you delve into those, you really need to do a gut check. So, we're going to break into small groups and do a little work on your core."

Kathy's raised eyebrows foreshadowed her question. "You mean like exercise and strengthening our core?"

"Well, it's a kind of exercise, but a workout for the mind—and since all of you know how I value core values, you should be very good at it."

CHAPTER 16

Sergio escorted Kathy and Carl up past the stand of pines where they'd taken their earlier break to a good-sized berm with a weathered picnic table. From there they had a panoramic view of the ranch and the surrounding mountains, all framed by powder blue skies.

"I've always liked this spot for thinking. And the walk up the hill clears my mind." Sergio said.

Carl nodded. "I like that about the ranch. It reduces the noise so you can see new perspectives. I mean, this is a world away from Madison."

"Yes," Kathy agreed. "Just like group practice is a world away from my current business model."

"Indeed," Sergio acknowledged. "Though, one of the things I hope this exercise shows you is that, at the core, the basis for doing your work as a dentist does not have to change. Structures will change, but if you align your core values with your partners, if you truly share a common purpose in a group practice, then you can create a solid foundation. That's what Sidney has always been about and it's no different if you're practicing solo or in a group—even more so in a group."

"That's reassuring," Carl said. "And you definitely planted the seed of possibility in starting a group practice together that Kathy and I are willing to explore, though we have no clue how to make that happen."

Sergio smiled. "The first step is being open to the possibility and what we're doing now is a second concrete step: having you and Kathy determine what conditions you need to have in place to fully commit and act."

They sat silently for a few moments considering those conditions before Carl spoke up. "One condition I know for sure is that everyone in the group would need to completely embrace and align behind the core values and purpose of the group."

"Have you and Kathy ever discussed your values with each other and what they mean?" Sergio asked.

Kathy and Carl looked at one another. "No," Kathy answered.

"Then that's the perfect place to begin. Articulate your core values as if they were the foundation of *your* group, a group you could be fully committed to and be willing to work for, like your own solo practice now."

"Then what?" asked Carl.

"Then you figure out the purpose of the group. The reason for its existence. Why it does what it does. What drives it? A purpose worthy of your time, money and energy. A purpose that would attract other dentists and staff to work for you. A purpose that patients would feel is in their best interest. A noble resolution. A vow you make that you will fulfill," Sergio explained, his eyes bright and voice animated.

Carl felt energized by Sergio's enthusiasm. "Is this how it worked for you when you got started?"

"Yes. It's what got me feeling that I could be a part of a group, if we shared the same values, purpose and mission. So, think of a dentist who has the same values, understands that the future is managed group, has a strong reputation, and might want to join you in forming a group practice.

"You also need to start thinking about a vision and a purpose. They must be big enough and real enough to inspire and empower you or you won't be able to handle the struggles, problems and breakdowns that will inevitably come in putting one of these together. Dentists who put groups together so they can avoid the future, or make a lot of money, or simply to protect the resale value of their practice, shouldn't form their own group. They should look for someone to acquire them. You've got to have a purpose bigger than any individual. You need to have a vision that is inspiring."

A cool breeze swept across the picnic table and Sergio's legal pad fluttered dramatically.

"I'm going to leave you two with this task: think about 'who' and think about a 'vision' you both could share in a group practice. You can stay here to do your thinking or," he pointed south, "I'd recommend the path just over the berm. It meets up with the river and follows it in a semi-circle winding back to the entrance to the ranch. I always find that walking refreshes my thinking and fuels my creativity. Any questions on the assignment before I leave you?"

"No," Carl said. "Kathy?"

"Not about this."

"Okay, then. Sidney would like us back in the main house by noon for lunch. If you do take the path, it's less than a mile, so you shouldn't have any trouble getting back on time."

"Thanks Sergio," Carl said. "Save a seat for us!"

Carl looked out to the river, then back to Kathy. "Up for a walk?"

"Sure," Kathy said with a smile. "It's so beautiful right here; I might find it hard to leave, ever, if I lived here full time. It's just breathtaking."

As they began walking down the hill towards the trail, Kathy turned to Carl. "You know, when Sergio asked us to think of dentists we both know in Wisconsin, anyone pop into your head?"

"Jim Boomer," Carl said not missing a beat.

"Me too!" Kathy exclaimed,

"Why do you think he came up for you?" Carl continued.

"Boomer's a great dentist," Kathy said. "Everyone I know really respects him and he's been through the Kois program, so we've got some common clinical background. I heard through the grapevine that he bought a practice in Fond du Lac. That would give us a little golden triangle, wouldn't it?"

"Yeah, I guess it would. Jim's an all-around great guy and a complete clinician. I can think of a couple other docs, but for the purposes of the exercise, maybe Jim is all we need right now?"

"Sure. So let's talk core values, shall we?"

The assignment Sergio had given them included core values and a purpose for a group practice. They needed to provide a simple definition for each value and a brief description of what the group would look like in one, three and five years. Forty minutes later they reached the entrance to the ranch and veered onto the driveway.

Without fully realizing it, Carl and Kathy were setting the foundation for a group practice that was a fit for both of them, and Jim Boomer. Whereas they'd been a little dazed and unresponsive a couple hours earlier, they were seeing the possibility in much greater detail. As if they were seeing it for the first time.

Fear of the future had morphed into a sense of greater purpose and a larger professional aspiration in just the space one morning on the ranch. Carl had to hand it to Sidney: he could still work his transformational magic.

CHAPTER 17

On the way to main house, they passed the bunkhouse. Carl stopped.

"On my first visit here, Sidney asked me to come down and join a meeting he was having with Richard and the other ranch hands. It really inspired me how Sidney and his team embraced their core values in prioritizing and getting their work done."

Just then the door to the bunkhouse opened and Richard stepped out. "Hey, Carl. Hey, Kathy. I saw you through the window. Is there something I can help you with?"

"Hi, Richard. Kathy and I were just heading back to the house and I was telling her about the meeting I sat in on when I was here before."

"I remember. Sidney wanted you to see how we run our day-to-day business. In fact, we just finished up a short weekly catch-up meeting. Would you like a cup of coffee? Our particular grind has a little more bite to it than the coffee in the main house."

"That sounds great," Kathy said. "It got a bit chilly on the last part of our walk."

"Great. Come on in."

Richard held the door as they filed in and then grabbed some mugs from the kitchenette. Kathy was drawn to the white board on the far wall.

"What's this list?" she asked, pointing at the white board.

"Carl may have already explained it to you, but it's our system," Richard began as he poured their coffees and took it to each of them. "That whiteboard is really the foundation of how we get work done around here: requests and promises. It represents our collaborative effort using requests and promises. I guess it's like staff huddles you have in your practices."

"Looks like it's got more detail, from what I can see," Kathy said. "You actually ask for time commitments?"

"Absolutely," Richard replied with a hint of fire in his eye that his stoic demeanor usually kept in check. "Any promise that doesn't include a 'by when' really has no teeth."

"Exactly," Carl said. "My experience at that meeting really opened my eyes. I took this system back to my office and, seriously, it was the simplest, most effective solution to getting things done I ever tried. And it worked immediately.

"I learned that I had pretty much lived in hope that staff would do what I asked for. I discovered that staff actually performed better when there was accountability," added Carl. "I even installed an extra-large white board on one wall of the break room so there was no place for any of us to hide. Eventually, it was also plastered with sticky notes of all colors. We now call it the APP. It stands for 'Action Plan for Performance.' Patients sometimes comment on the board when they walk by. They want to know what we're up to."

"That's why we've done it this way for years. We know we can't run this ranch without communication, cooperation and commitment," Richard explained. "Early on, Sidney taught us that commitment shows up in your checkbook and your calendar, and it didn't take long to figure out that it was going to make our work easier, by putting it on a calendar and holding to it."

"Did you get much resistance from your crew?" asked Kathy. "I'm thinking I might get some reluctance from my staff, even though it seems to make a lot of sense."

"Kathy, we don't really look at it that way. It works. We know it makes a big difference, not just for the ranch, but for each of us individually. And if anyone at any time begins to resist, well, we've got the wrong guy. If you think you have a staff member who would complain, I suspect you might also have a nagging feeling about them being a fit in your practice as well?"

Kathy screwed up her face as she took that in.

Carl added, "When I came back from Taos last time and wanted to institute these changes, my office manager wouldn't get on board and I ended up letting her go. After my staff got over the shock of Sharon leaving, they realized I was committed to requests and promises and they had no problem with using the system. Quickly they embraced it, and they're the ones who turned it into 'the APP' and ran with it."

"It is an excellent tool for change, Kathy," Richard said. "When Carl was here the first time it was as plain as a tick on a dog that he was determined to create the best dental practice he could. But he had given over his practice to someone else to run, and lost himself in the process. *Your practice is your vision, manifested.* If it's not producing the results you expect, then something is in the way, and that 'something' may be you."

Kathy extended her hand to Richard. "It's easy to see why Sidney places so much trust in you to run the ranch. You sound just like him and I mean that as a compliment."

"It would be hard to take it any other way, Ma'am. Thank you."

Carl glanced at his watch. "We better get going, Kathy. Thanks for the coffee. I might be back for some of this cowboy grind of yours; I like it."

"Help yourself, Carl. Anytime. You two have a good afternoon. Enjoy your lunch. I know Dawn picked up some great peppers at the market this morning, if you are feeling adventurous."

CHAPTER 18

Carl did sample Dawn's roasted peppers at lunch along with her Taos potato salad and bulging pulled pork sandwiches. The peppers definitely had a zing, so he drank plenty of iced sun tea, but they didn't leave Carl sweating as much as thoughts of how he'd work in a group practice.

After lunch, Sidney gathered them in front of the fireplace in the Great Room.

"How was the walk, Kathy? Carl? It's beautiful out along the river there, isn't it?" Sidney asked.

Kathy chuckled. "To tell the truth, I remember the view from the hill, but once Carl and I got to talking about our group core values, I don't recall the scenery much at all. We got pretty engrossed in the group idea.

"Then Carl took me by the bunk house and we ran into Richard. He showed me your system of requests and promises. He's really on top of it."

"Yes he is," Sidney agreed. "I've always found it worthwhile to pay close attention to what Richard has to say."

Sidney turned to the whole group. "So, getting back to your group values assignment. Hopefully, it reminded you that a weak core leads to reduced strength and possible injury. It's the same in forming a group. This is one of the biggest mistakes dentists make. They think if they get the structure right, you know, the list of 'what to do and how to do it,' the group will function automatically. But, unless the group members are aligned with their values, the group will not have the cohesion to last when difficult decisions have to be made."

"I'm beginning to understand that idea," Carl said. "I'm also feeling the same spark you ignited last time I was here."

Sidney looked at Carl with a hint of pride. "Glad you are starting to replace that trepidation with possibility. Remember, this group approach is not just a fix to keep your practice solvent; it's actually a better way to practice dentistry. The synergy you can create within a group committed to the health of their patients and their community far exceeds what you can accomplish on your own as a solo dentist. Having seen quite a few groups form, I can tell you that they always get to the point where they understand just how much more satisfying it is to work with peers to create something incredible. They're no longer in competition, they're in collaboration. What's critical to any successful group is that everyone be committed to the same future."

"How does that look?" Vinny asked.

"Good question," Sergio chimed in. "Vinny, you are always living into a future and it is the future that determines your actions in the present. When people don't share a common future they take actions that are not always aligned or coherent. That's the essential feature of an authentic vision. It is shared future. A future that people are committed to achieving."

"Keep going," Vinny prompted.

"Ultimately a vision is a future, a special kind of future. Martin Luther King, John Kennedy, Gandhi, all great leaders speak about a future. Not a pie-in-the-sky future. Not a past-based future. But a future that is possible. A future that isn't about themselves, but about making a lasting difference. A vision is a future, about a future, that is for a future, that's not about you, a future that's clearly possible, a future that will leave a legacy."

"Whoa," Steve interrupted. "What does that mean exactly? I'm sorry, that sounds too, I dunno, something... Does it have to be so complicated?"

"I think I get it." Vinny told Steve. "A vision is a future, and this future is something that will make a difference. This future, this vision, describes a future that stands for something that people, staff, whomever, can see is possible to achieve. It's a future that isn't about me alone, but about the people this future will impact. How's that?"

Steve was still looking at Vinny and clearly thinking about his summary. "You know, I always wanted to be the best at what I do, to make a difference. Maybe I just don't want to accept this group idea as the answer, but it's starting to sound a lot like what I do personally, could be made to work in a group of folks."

Sidney held up his arms expansively. "You can see that there is a lot at stake in how you see your legacy. Steve, you're seeing a glimpse now. And that's all we're trying to accomplish here. Stay open to the possibility that a group could compliment your own personal vision, Okay?"

Steve nodded and Sidney continued, "Let's see how each of you addressed the group values assignment prior to lunch. We want to hear what you came up with. Kathy, let's start with you and Carl."

Kathy took out her notes. "Our core values are in the order we came up with them. They're not polished yet, but we think they capture our intent and feeling."

1. **Integrity**: We are honest. We do what we say we will do. We honor our word.
2. **Courage**: We have the courage to do the right thing simply because it's the right thing to do.
3. **Respect**: We treat our patients and each other the way we would like to be treated.
4. **Excellence**: We strive for excellence in all we do. Good enough isn't good enough.
5. **Improvement**: We strive to get better at what we do every day.
6. **Service**: We are here to serve our patients at a level higher than they have ever experienced.

7. **Profit**: It's absolutely necessary that we are profitable. Without profit, we can serve no one or fund the future."

Kathy paused and then explained. "What Carl and I realized was if we truly committed to these values in our group, it would be a group we would not only want to be part of, but other dentists would as well. We also agreed that if these values were fully embraced, it's a group that staff would want to work for, and patients would want to come to."

"Thank you, Kathy," Sidney said. "That was right on target. Clear and focused. A great foundation for a group practice. Well done. The reason this is so important is that most groups are formed without real clarity or sincerity about core values. They may focus on the money and security. Or increasing the multiple of their EBITDA (earnings before interest, taxes, depreciation and amortization) and the stock value. A group can focus too narrowly on increasing the accumulated worth by adding more practices too quickly. It's imperative to keep in mind that a group without clear values is a boat without a rudder.

"Values decide how you decide. Values tell you what to say 'No' to and what to say 'Yes' to. Values lead you to the right practices to acquire. Values tell you what kind of dentists to recruit, same with staff. Values are the lenses through which you see the world. And how you see the world determines what kind of actions you take. Values determine what kind of relationships you sustain and which ones you discard."

Sidney grew impassioned as he finished. "When core values exist as platitudes, neither honored nor upheld, the core of the group is weak and shallow. The group lacks the necessary energy to effectively confront challenges and take powerful actions. It is fundamental and critical for group success that the dentists, executives and staff respect and faithfully adhere to the core values – period. Does everyone get that? Steve?"

"Yes. I see it," Steve said. "I'm really going to need a beer at the end of this day, but, yeah, it's making more sense to me now."

"Okay. Now, Kathy, what did you come up with for the purpose of your group?"

"We wanted something short and aspirational and we think we hit it with: *Extraordinary people delivering extraordinary care.*"

"I like the simplicity and brevity. What does that phrase mean to you and Carl?" Sidney asked.

"Well, Carl and I decided we didn't want to form a group that was just better than every other group. We wanted something that totally fit our core values. Carl and I have spent years training to be good clinicians. We've spent thousands of dollars, hundreds of hours, getting very good at diagnosis, treatment planning and clinical delivery. We wanted a purpose that would continue to drive us every day, push us to go above and beyond. We wanted a purpose that would inspire us, one that would stimulate and encourage us and our staffs. We wanted a purpose we would be willing to go pedal to the metal for and a purpose that would attract dentists who gave everything they could to be great, to be extraordinary.

"We don't mean 'extraordinary' in a boastful or arrogant way. We want to convey extraordinary in terms of our values; integrity, courage, excellence, service, and respect. If we truly embrace these values, although we are ordinary people, we could be extraordinary in our efforts. We would need to be committed to providing extraordinary dentistry, with an extraordinary team, with an extraordinary organization."

Carl felt a lot of pride and satisfaction listening to Kathy. If they could develop a group that matched what she was saying, it would be *extraordinary*. He decided that was a group practice he could really be committed to.

"You are really starting to coalesce around a strong purpose," Sergio said. "What were you able to come up with in terms of the 1, 3 and 5-year plan? Carl, will you tell us about that?"

Kathy handed Carl their notes. "Sure. I'll admit we're more unclear about how this looks, since we don't know what it will take to do this, but here's what we came up with. Let us know if we are on the mark or going in the totally wrong direction.

"Our first year is adding another dentist immediately to our team and…"

Sidney held up a hand. "Sorry to interrupt, Carl, but start with the 5-year future. We want to begin with the future you envision and then work backwards to today. Don't go from today forward. Go from the future backwards. Tell me where you see your group in five years?"

"Well, all right," Carl scanned down their notes. "This is probably going to sound a little crazy, but we envision 25 practices merged together under one brand. And by the way, we came up with a name for our group, *Superior Dental Centers*. You know, after Lake Superior, of course, and because we both want this dental group to be wonderful, astonishing, and *extraordinary*.

"Anyway, in five years Superior Dental will have 25 locations throughout the Madison-Milwaukee-Fond du Lac triangle. We have a colleague with a practice in Fond du Lac we both really like and think he's a good fit for us. And it creates a geographic 'triangle,' so the logo will have a triangle in it.

"Each practice will be doing over one million dollars in revenue. We'll form a specialty group consisting of perio, endo, and oral surgery that will serve all the offices as needed. We'll have our own CE programs, but will make sure that all dentists adhere to the Kois principles. We'll only acquire practices and have dentists that have been through or are going to go through Kois training. All associates after the first year or so would be required to go to Seattle as well. Kathy and I feel that we need to have a consistent diagnostic and treatment planning philosophy. We also talked about having weekly group Skype calls to discuss difficult cases. Also, the same practice management software, whatever that turns out to be."

"Do you realize you're talking about this group as it 'will' happen?" Sidney piped in.

"I guess I am," Carl replied, surprised. "It all feels really possible when you work with a partner who has the same view of the future. I mean, we're having fun, but it's kind of exciting at the same time."

"Exactly right!" Sidney encouraged. "You're talking like a large national company with CE programs and orientations, clinical training, and diagnostic protocols. Plus having the same software so each practitioner utilizes the same diagnostic sequences. You might also consider mentors and small study groups that work on cases together so dentists come to clinical alignment over time."

"Mentors would be a good idea," Carl noted. "Well, that's our thinking so far. We're still fuzzy on how the company would be formed, the corporate structure, how the management team would be set up to manage 25 practices, how we'd finance the company, but we are clear on the values, purpose and vision."

"That's where you have to start," Sidney said. "During the break before dinner I suggest Sergio work with you and Kathy on exactly what it will look like and feel like to walk into a Superior Dental location. Be as specific as possible. If you can imagine it, you can make it real."

Sidney turned to Vinny and Steve. "I'll work with you two on your five year plan. A reminder that dinner tonight is here at the main house at 7:00. Dawn is cooking a traditional pueblo meal of elk stew, blue corn on the cob with a southwestern salad. We'll also have 'fry bread,' which is flat bread made of corn flour, and a hot drink called 'masa' made of blue corn flour, cane sugar, vanilla, and cinnamon. It'll be a memorable meal."

Sidney paused. "And after dinner we have a special event planned. I'm betting it'll be even more unforgettable."

"Sidney, you are a man of mystery," Carl commented.

"Mystery helps whet our appetite for adventure. And that's what all this is about. An exploration, a trek, a journey, an adventure into group practice. Only the brave need apply. Let's be brave!"

CHAPTER 19

As Kathy, Carl and Sergio walked past the kitchen entry, they were momentarily drawn in by the aroma of cornbread just out of the oven. Dawn motioned them over with a conspiratorial wave. "You want a sample?" she asked.

"Absolutely," Kathy said. "Food for our expedition into group practice."

Sergio laughed. "Yes. It'll take a lot of energy and imagination."

"In that case, I might need two pieces," Carl said.

Fortified with Dawn's melt-in-your-mouth cornbread, the three made their way to the picnic table where they'd met earlier in the day.

"You know, Carl, the more I think about it the more I think we can pull this off," Kathy told him. "I'm getting more excited about the possibility. How about you? What are you thinking?"

"Honestly, I find myself vacillating. One minute I'm excited as all get out, the next I get nervous. It's overwhelming to think of all that would go into forming a group practice, and, you know me, I'm pretty cautious. There are a lot of unanswered questions. I like things buttoned down. I like to follow a proven formula. It scares me to not have all the answers."

Sergio had been listening to their exchange and spoke up. "That's the difference between an entrepreneurial dentist and one who is not. It's their willingness to take a risk."

Sergio looked directly at Carl now. "There are no sure things, Carl. I was very much like you. My tendency at the time was to wait until others had tried it. But it just kept on gnawing at me, and, in the end, I couldn't overlook the possibility that if I didn't get ahead of these changes, I might be left behind. So I felt I had to take the risk."

"But I'm concerned that we don't have the ability, the knowledge, or the skill-set to pull this off."

"Entrepreneurs are willing to try and fail whereas most dentists do whatever they can to avoid failing. But, let me state the obvious. You're here, right? You came to Taos knowing that you needed to take some action. That shows that you are more proactive, more of a risk taker than you think."

"I get that, but I don't want to fail and lose," Carl admitted. "The risk of coming to listen to Sidney isn't the same as setting up a multi-million dollar group practice."

"Agreed. But entrepreneurs don't see themselves as 'failures' when an idea doesn't work out. While some dentists who fail might think they are a failure. If you avoid taking risks because you might fail then it's all about you and your ego and you avoid taking risks. If the risk is about a bigger idea, an enterprise whose time you believe has come, then it's about the idea and inspiration, and you'll risk more and fight harder for a thing bigger than yourself.

"That's one of the reasons I believe managed group practices are growing like weeds. Dentists, because they are afraid to risk, have created a vacuum that is being filled by dentist and non-dentist entrepreneurs. Given all the forces we've spoken about today, the future is managed group practices. First movers, early adopters, people who will risk the risk will reap the reward."

"Carl, we said that 'courage' is one of our group core values. And Sidney told us we needed to be brave, so here's a test of that value," Kathy said.

"That's right. Okay, no guts no glory." Carl looked at Sergio. "Where do we go from here?"

"Your task now is to really envision Superior Dental. What will a Superior Dental office look and feel like when you walk through the door? You said earlier that you wanted your core values to be in full view. You wanted Superior Dental to be extraordinary. So, describe the office, the staff, the doctors and the interactions. Get as granular as you can. Imagine every aspect of it. See it clearly. Got it?"

"I think we do," Kathy replied.

Carl nodded. "Yes."

"Great. Then I'll leave you to your work."

Sergio headed back down to the main house. As Carl watched him go, he realized that he had reached his 'tipping point.' He was ready to dig in. He still didn't know what it all meant, but he was ready to try. Carl didn't think that dentists were all that risk adverse—he'd played poker with enough of them. They were just professionals who really enjoyed what they did and the challenge of creating healthy smiles and happy patients. Stepping into a bigger arena and taking on more responsibility, could be intimidating for anyone in any profession.

You just had to really see the possibility. That's what Sidney was so good at. Helping him get past the trepidation and channeling that negative energy into excitement and positive action to create a dental business that really matched his values and his aspirations for the future.

"Where do you want to begin?" Kathy asked.

"One step at time," Carl said. "One step at a time."

CHAPTER 20

Carl was back in his room staring out the window at an eagle gliding high above the ranch. He was experiencing a little de ja vu. He had been here before, wondering about the future of his practice, wondering if he was tough enough to make the changes he needed to secure his future.

The afternoon laying out Superior Dental with Kathy had helped his frame of mind. They'd been able to knock out a rough framework for the kind of group practice that they could really invest their heart in. But, when he came back to his room to have a brief rest and get ready for dinner, some of his self doubt returned. Could he really do this? Did he have it in him?

Then he thought of Veronica and he realized how much he missed her at times like these. He got out his phone and called. She picked up on the second ring.

"Hey honey, it's your Taos troublemaker. I know you're probably heading to the school fundraiser soon. Just wanted to touch base real quick."

"Well, Mr. Troublemaker, all is peaceful here on the Oldquist home front. Especially, because all my gourmet cupcakes are finished for the event. So, how are things at the ranch? Has Sidney convinced you to run for President yet?"

Carl laughed. "In some ways that seems easier. Let me bring you up to speed on what's been happening." So, Carl filled her in about the group practice approach and how she and Kathy Germain had been seriously looking at what that might mean to build a group practice with Jim Boomer. He tried to be as upbeat and positive about what he'd learned, but Veronica heard something else.

"Okay, Carl, what's really going on? You're spinning this all positive, but I can hear a note of reluctance in that sweet voice of yours."

Carl didn't even try to hem or haw. "Well, Veronica, nothing gets by you when it comes to me. Of course, I'm reluctant. This is huge. It means a ton of change and investment without any guarantee of success."

"Okay. What are you worried about specifically?"

"This group practice stuff is like another world. It's seems very complex, so much to understand and get accomplished. I'm not sure I can do it all."

"But it's called *group practice*, so you're in a group, right. You said you'd be working with Kathy and Jim. Doesn't that mean you'd share the burden and the tasks with them?"

"Yes, but…" Carl started but trailed off in sudden realization. He was still thinking like a solo doc. That it was all on him. Yes he understood the concept of a group practice and shared responsibility and accountability, but he had not embraced what that would mean. Others to share the load. A team approach. Requests and promises.

"Veronica," he began, "you are a genius. Just like last time when the practice was tanking you helped me see that you and I were in it together. That it wasn't all on my shoulders. Now, you're reminding me again. Only I'll have you and two other committed docs to share the load."

"I was always good at math, sweetie," Veronica teased.

"You're also good at people—especially your husband and helping him change his mindset in a positive way."

"Years of experience. So, sounds like we might have some big things to talk about when you get back tomorrow evening? I'll make sure I have a special dinner and some good wine for the conversation."

"You bet. We are just in the idea and learning phase here, but you've helped me hurl another barrier—namely, my own stubborn thinking as a solo doc."

"You don't need to apologize for caring about your practice," Veronica said. "Just give yourself time to really understand what the changes would mean. Get a clear picture of the challenges and then we'll tackle them together."

Together. The word tingled down Carl's spine. He relaxed. It was clear that if he got the right people together, a real team, it could get done. And with

Kathy, an all-star organizer in her own right, it would be like having the Michael Jordan of organization on their team. Jim Boomer too—a clinician's clinician if ever there was one.

And, of course, Veronica. She would always be his most valuable person. If she was on board anything seemed possible.

"You're a lifesaver, sweetie. Thanks for helping me put two and two together."

"Always. I can hear in your voice that wheels are spinning in a more positive direction, and that's good because I've got to get these cupcakes rolling towards the fundraiser."

"Absolutely. Thanks, Ronnie. Have a good time. You're amazing and I love you."

"I love you, too, Carl. Keep learning down there and I'll see you tomorrow evening."

Carl hung up. He went back to the window. The eagle was still circling in the deepening sky. The great bird was hunting. Looking for an opportunity to pounce on. There was no certainty that it would find a meal, its sustenance, but it was a strong, resilient creature, hardwired to keep at it.

Carl knew he needed to keep that persevering mindset to figure out if he could make a group practice work. And he knew he had something on his side that even the mighty eagle soaring out there didn't have. He had support. He had others looking out for him. He wasn't alone. First and foremost, he had Veronica and, if he chose, he had Kathy and possibly Jim Boomer as partners, and then Sidney and Sergio as mentors to help them get their group practice started.

It was high time Carl started thinking like he was part of a team.

CHAPTER 21

Carl sat stunned, staring into the bonfire that had been the center of the ceremony he had just watched along with Kathy, Vinny, Steve, Sergio and Sidney. This was the surprise Sidney had arranged. An opportunity for them to attend a tribal dance of Richard's pueblo. It was spectacular and under the piercing stars of the high desert, it felt ancient and timeless.

Vinny leaned over to Carl. "Wow. And I thought I'd seen good shows in Vegas. This was ten times as good—and this felt spiritual. I don't know how I'll be able to describe it to my wife and family."

"I know what you mean," Carl said. "Kind of like a high mass under the stars."

"Reverent and stunning," Kathy added. "It gave me chills."

Steve silently nodded. He seemed to be deep in thought.

"That's why I wanted you to be here," Sidney said. "You need to remember how deep your core values take you. What you watched and experienced here has to do with Richard's tribe and what they believe and how they want to be in the world."

As if on cue, Richard emerged from the darkness on the other side of the bonfire with an armful of wood. He tossed the load onto the dwindling fire which exploded with sparks popping like fireworks and spiraling high into the night sky.

Richard then came and squatted across from the group of dentists. "Thank you for coming. I hope you found the evening interesting."

"It was amazing," Kathy offered. "The dance seemed to tell a story."

"Yes. This ceremony is a history of our tribe," Richard explained. "It's all about the change we have experienced as a people. We know well from centuries of change that we cannot escape change. We must embrace it.

"And the only way to embrace change is keep your values present and constant. That is how my tribe has survived the turmoil of change: our values are our backbone, our strength, our essence. They have kept us together and alive for thousands of years. Our values are enshrined in our ceremonies, in our religion, in our elders. Even our dances, our chanting, our drumming, are our values spoken.

"Our love of the land and its inhabitants, our respect for our elders and the spirits of our ancestors. We acknowledge daily gratitude, giving thanks to the Great Spirit for all the good we have in our lives. It is our connectedness that gives us strength and appreciation. When we lose sight of these values, we lose ourselves and dishonor our history. This has happened to many tribes, many people within tribes. It is terrible to watch."

Richard paused and Carl was drawn to his eyes which burned with intensity greater than the bonfire at his back. "Even though I am working on the ranch here with Sidney and members of my family, my values, my respect for the land and my people has not changed. My values sustain me no matter what changes occur around me.

"Change can be hard, but when you think too much about change, you can allow fear to paralyze you and suspend all possibility."

Without looking up, Richard pointed to the stars overhead. "Billions of dreams and possibilities surround us. They are limitless. If you can master your fear of the unknown or untried then your possibilities expand. Here at the Ranch, there is nobody who will tell you, *It is impossible.* There is no one who will ask, *What if you fail?* There is only you and possibility. Nothing more."

Richard stood up and nodded to each of them and then headed back into the darkness to rejoin his tribe.

After a few moments, Sidney spoke up. "Like Richard said I cannot make you see possibility. But always want you to believe that you can open the door to it. It is there for you to have if you wish it.

"Richard has a long and storied history of his people. It helps sustain them through the challenges of change. To build a lasting group practice, you need to create your story, base it on your values and live it."

Steve, so quiet during the evening asked, "How do we do that, Sidney?"

Sidney stood and went over to where the drums and tambourines used for the ceremony had been left. He picked up a drum and beat on it slowly. "Join me. Join each other. Take a risk. Start with a moment and let it grow."

Carl stared at Sidney, peacefully drumming in the roar of the fire. He felt frozen. Was this right? It seemed too far out of his comfort zone. But, then, Kathy stood up and joined him with a tambourine. Sergio went and picked up a drum, and then Vinny and Steve. Only Carl was left. He still didn't know why he was so afraid.

Then he felt a presence at his side. It was Dawn, and Richard was behind her.

"Don't you want to join in?" Dawn asked.

Carl felt like a little kid.

"Come on. We'll do it together," Dawn said leading him over. Richard handed him a drum. Richard began to chant and Dawn helped Carl take up the beat.

In a matter of moments, Carl felt the beat himself and let it take him. Off the distant canyon walls the sound came back and welcomed him. He was mesmerized by Richard's chant and the music of the group. They were together. Making a moment. Maybe one that could launch a new future.

Overhead, the stars shone bright with possibility.

CHAPTER 22

Even though they'd stayed up late and communed under the Milky Way, the conversation was animated as they gathered for breakfast. Carl was on his third cup of coffee and deep into a conversation with Sergio.

"So what does it look like to be a leader in a group practice? I mean, in my practice, it has to be me. But leading other dentists and their staffs, I'm not sure how that would work."

"Carl," Sergio began, "here's what I found when I went the group practice route. What I believed about my own practice, I found that other dentists pretty much believed the same thing about theirs. So, when we banded together, we formed a tribe. Kind of what we saw in action last night with the Taos Pueblo ceremony. Whereas the Pueblo divides into councils, our group practice divided into a board and several committees. And since we all believed in the same thing, had very similar core values, there was a level of trust among us that we could, and would, make good decisions for everyone involved."

"I get that. But what about working with non-dentists? I've heard plenty of horror stories about CEOs and other senior executives of managed groups. How do you deal with that?"

Sidney, who'd been listening as he spread jam on one of Dawn's fresh muffins, joined the conversation, "You choose, Carl. You choose the person who understands and embraces your group's core values, your purpose and your mission. You're not looking for a job description; you're looking for a partner. There are great executives out there who want to partner with dentists and want what you want. I am sure there are terrible ones as well, but those aren't the ones you'll hire."

"How do you know who to hire?"

"Before you can determine the kind of people you need, you and Kathy have to have a very clear vision for Superior Dental."

Kathy leaned into the conversation. "Well, if Carl and I started Superior Dental and brought on Jim Boomer as our third partner, I believe we'd have a solid foundation because I know in my heart we believe the same thing about patient care and dentistry and we hold the same core values."

"That's essential," Sergio acknowledged. "If you truly believe you can create a managed group practice that delivers on its vision and faithfully abides by its core values, you have a very strong chance of succeeding."

"Given that, Kathy and Carl, what do you think Superior Dental will look like in five years? Sidney asked.

"Okay, like I said, 25 practices in the golden triangle, Madison-Milwaukee-Fond du Lac," Carl explained. "Our Superior Dental dentists would have the same core values as we do, they'd be part of a managed group practice that works well. We'd be committed to the group's success, doing the best technical dentistry possible, providing the best patient care possible. Walking into any Superior Dental clinic would not be identical, like McDonalds. Each clinic would have certain shared design elements, but each would have its own character."

"Exactly," Kathy said. "And, I think, given our geography and our communities, people will want individual providers, so each provider should have their own location, their name at the top in the beginning. Perhaps with a second line 'A Superior Dental Provider' under their name. We wouldn't let anybody in that didn't have our values, didn't do a ton of CE, or wasn't a good dentist."

Sidney chuckled. "Look at how far your thinking has come since breakfast yesterday. Not only have you acknowledged the possibility that a group practice might be the way forward in dentistry, but you are already envisioning what it would like for you in your locale. All that thinking will provide the framework for our work today and you'll both get so much more."

"This'll be exciting, but we've got a lot to do, so eat up," Sidney encouraged as he finished his muffin.

CHAPTER 23

Once breakfast was finished and cleared, Sidney launched into the work for the day. "Yesterday was about accessing the heart and soul of a group practice, its core values, its purpose, the look and feel that would make it worthwhile for you to pursue this.

"Today, we'll be painting group practice in very broad brush strokes. We cannot get specific given the multitude of variations of managed group practices. As we have said before, if you've seen one, you've only seen one. Unlike solo practice, where for the most part it looks, feels and operates the same, managed groups are entrepreneurial expressions, so each one is unique in its own way."

"I don't want a cookie cutter approach to forming a group practice, but is there some kind of formula?" Vinny asked.

"Again, we come back to the difference between an entrepreneur and most dentists. Most dentists are satisfied with recipes, formulas, step-by-step checklists for doing things. That could explain the plethora of practice management consultants all selling essentially the same thing, and for the most part, doing the same thing. Although they attest to being different, they focus on the standards of solo practice and use similar systems to achieve results. That's because solo practice is more, better or slightly different of the same thing.

"An entrepreneur has a vision, a future that he or she is committed to achieving and starts there and works backwards. There are lots of gaps, unanswered elements that will need to be solved. An entrepreneur says, 'I'll figure it out when I get there' and that is the biggest difference between an entrepreneur and your average dentist. The typical dentist needs to know the answer beforehand, they need to know if it has been done before, how many times, and finally if it will work. Entrepreneurs simply say, 'We'll figure it out.'"

Sergio tag teamed. "It's really about the vision, purpose, and core values. Our five dentists who had known each other for 15 or more years sat down with a facilitator and we knew after the session pretty much what we wanted our group to look like, at least after the first five years. How many practices, what kind of dentists, and approximate locations. We also knew "why" we were doing it, we had our purpose. We knew what we wanted to convey to our communities, so we basically had our brand. We began by organizing ourselves as a board of directors, and laid out the vision on paper."

"Can you give a little more detail, Sergio?" Steve asked.

"Sure. We said we wanted 'X' number of practices by the end of year 5. Then we knew how many we needed by year 4, year, 3, year 2 and the first year. Then we had to figure out our corporate structure so as best to fit our values and vision. We hired an attorney. He asked a lot of questions for which we had few answers. So we retained the attorney and the board addressed and eventually answered the questions. That brought our group to an entirely new level. The attorney asked about future ownership, the kind of partnerships we wanted, the kind of company we wanted to be, and so on."

Sergio paused and then added. "You see, Steve, how you get there is an evolution, it's not turnkey, it's not prescribed. Each time we answered the attorney's questions we learned more about who we wanted to be. The power lives in the question, not in the answers."

"I have a question," Carl said. "Should you have every practice under one roof, one name, or separate individual entities for each practice location? Like Kathy mentioned, I'd like to keep my name on the door. But what works best?"

"Good question, Carl," Sergio said. "In the beginning we thought it would be best to keep our names as well, remain as separate entities. This had to do with our thinking that each practice had an established identity, a local brand, a certain cache in the doctor's name, and it would be lost if it was changed to the name of the company. Just like you and Kathy said about Superior Dental. Well, knowing what I know now, particularly about where the future is going, brand will be far more important and powerful than any individual name. An easy example is the Mayo

Clinic versus Dr. John Smith. By the end of the decade brands will dominate the market. Heartland and Clear Choice are great examples of that today.

"You know getting dentists to play as a team rather than a group is cardinal to success. That's one of the greatest failures I see, is dentists not moving from group to team."

"Why is that?" asked Vinny.

"Dentists are smart, capable, self-driven professionals. They like their independence. They like to be in control. So much so they have their professional associations rallying against the scourge of 'corporate dental practice.' Most dentists, at this time, consider managed group practice a menace and continue to reaffirm solo practice, fee-for-service, individual control over all services provided."

Sidney startled them by asking, "What kind of dentistry would dentists provide if they were salaried and not paid on production? Check out the Cleveland Clinic, their physicians are salaried. This approach encompasses what is best for the group, not the individual. In essence it becomes a team expression, not an individual expression. And that is where dentistry is headed as well."

"Sidney, what's the difference between group and team?" Kathy asked.

"Well, simply put, most managed group practices operate as a group. A group is very different than a team. Individuals participate in a group to achieve their own personal goals and agenda. Belonging to a group enhances an individual's success through the group's resources, relationships with other members and the multitude of networks made available as extensions of the group. A team, on the other hand, is about team success, not individual success.

"In my experience, groups tend to fracture under duress, whereas teams unite under pressure. Groups sidestep difficult conversations while teams step right into them. The intention of their speaking is different. Groups talk the talk. Teams walk the talk.

Sergio jumped in. "You want to play on a team. Being from Texas, we love the San Antonio Spurs because they play as a team and that's how they win. Team beats superstars every time."

"So, how do you convert a group into a team?" Carl asked.

"The natural state when people are coalesced into a unit identified by their skill set, their background of experience, and their previous track record is 'group.' Moving to 'team' is not a how, it is a who. And that 'who' is leadership. Without leadership, team does not occur. Leadership is the glue that brings individuals together in a group and generates the phenomenon of team. That's why these managed groups put together by equity partner investors, thinking they can simply roll up practices and succeed consistently fails. They don't recruit powerful dentist leadership which would make all the difference.

"When you look at the big successful managed group practices you will always, and I mean always, find great leadership, not just in the founder, CEO or president, but in their executive teams and directors. Leadership converts group to team and teams are far better performers than groups.

"I think at this point, what we've been talking about is solo or two person ownership of multiple locations. Once you are successful at several practices, you are poised to take the next step. Leadership development is where you are ready to turn it into a business."

Sidney paused and looked around the table. "I can see by your expressions that you need to digest this for a bit. Let's take a half hour break. Get some air and we'll get back to this at 10:30."

CHAPTER 24

"Let's walk down to the river and debrief," Carl suggested to Kathy.

"Sounds good," Kathy replied.

A brisk pace got them to the water's edge in less than ten minutes. They stood on the bank of the river, a branch of the Rio Grande whose source originated in the San Juan Mountain range in Colorado. For several moments they just stood and watched the river flow by.

Carl recalled a conversation he'd had with Richard at this very spot five years earlier. He told Kathy that Richard's most memorable comment at the time had been, "If you lose your values, you forget who you are."

"He kind of said that again, in different words yesterday in the bunkhouse," Kathy said. *Your practice is your vision, manifested. If you're not getting the results you expect, it might be you, it might be your vision.*"

"Exactly. I called Veronica before dinner yesterday and she made me realize that I'm still looking at this as if I'm the one who has to get everything done. I'm still thinking with a solo doctor mentality instead of understanding that a group of us will be contributing together."

"For me," Kathy said, "I'm starting to get the feeling that there is another gear I haven't been considering. A group makes sense to me and I think working in a group setting would be amazing. But I'm starting to understand that there's a bigger vision that can be accomplished by a group of like-minded dentists and staff, something much bigger than me and my solo practice could ever achieve. I think about the Mayo Clinic, the Cleveland Clinic, Scripts, you know. I can be a part of something just like that."

"Yeah," Carl acknowledged. "Something bigger than ourselves."

Something upriver caught Carl's eye. He turned and about 150 yards away he saw a figure on horseback crossing the river. The rider was dressed in traditional Native American clothing. His horse was adorned in colorful blankets. Carl motioned to Kathy and they both stared.

"Is that Richard?" she asked.

Carl squinted and shielded his eyes from the sun dancing on the river. The rider appeared almost iridescent, a mirage of a shaman or a medicine man. "I think it's him."

Then the rider waved to them and they knew it was Richard. He looked like he'd been doing this for a thousand years, looking over the land, gauging the ebb and flow of the river and the life it fed.

Carl was struck by the image and how Richard's connection to the land represented a future that had always existed for him and his tribe. A people affected by the constant change around them, yet able to stay true to their beliefs and values.

In that moment, it finally hit home for Carl. He could adapt to any environment, if he stayed true to his core values. He could build a new practice with other docs if they shared the same values. That's where Sidney and Richard were leading him.

But, like the proverbial horse, only Carl could drink the water—or in this case take the group practice plunge.

Carl waved back to Richard and then turned to Kathy. "Do you remember the quote: *No man ever steps in the same river twice, for it's not the same river and he's not the same man?*

"Vaguely. What are you thinking?"

"Kathy, I was here five years ago to learn where I'd gone wrong. Now, I'm back facing a big shift in how we do business. I don't want to have to face it, but that's the key. There's really no choice. The river will keep flowing whether I'm swimming against the current or with it. It sure makes more sense to go with it and harness the power of the river."

"So, I guess that means were about to step into the river?" Kathy asked.

"I suppose it does. And it'll change us and the way we do business in a big way—a good way."

CHAPTER 25

When they reconvened at 10:30, Sidney opened with a story about the addition they'd added to the ranch. "When we decided we were getting busy enough to add another building, more of a separate meeting center, really, we wrote down every single thing we wanted. I had brought in a large white board to write our ideas on. The process of using the white board and mapping out the functionality we wanted in the Center led us to 'thinking maps.' I'm guessing you've probably heard of these."

"Sounds like the APP my staff developed to monitor requests and promises," Carl volunteered.

"That's right. We ultimately added a second white board because we needed more space for our thoughts and inadvertently created a 3-dimensional thinking map and that generated some really interesting results. There was just something about a physical expression of the Center that really brought it to life."

"Nifty idea," Vinny said.

"Well, we actually took it a little farther than that. We knew we'd be working with emerging groups at the Center and we saw so much promise in this planning tool that we included a thinking map room."

"An entire room?" asked Kathy. "Really?"

"Exactly. Let's go see it and, better yet, use it, to take the next step in envisioning your group practice." Sidney popped up like a Jack in the Box.

They all followed him as he led the way outside and down to the meeting center entrance. They passed through the heavy oak door into the large meeting space. From there they were led around the corner to a hallway and then into a room on the left. As they entered, on the far side of the room there was a set of huge French doors opened out into a landscaped courtyard. Beyond that was wide open space.

As beautiful as it was, when they pried their eyes free of the view, the remaining three walls of the 'thinking map' room were covered in white board material from about waist high all the way to the ceiling. In the middle of the room was a long oak table, which might have been mistaken for a big dining table were it not for multiple cans filled with markers, stacks of Post Its of all colors and multi-colored index cards. It was a work table with plenty of room to spread out. A light fixture hung on heavy steel chains above the table, the length of the work surface. A folding ladder stood in the corner, at the ready for making use of the higher real estate on the walls. The room was simple, and clearly designed for a single purpose. Thinking. Ideas. Possibility.

"What do you think?" Sidney asked like a proud father.

"Amazing," Carl offered. "I mean, this is our APP on steroids!"

Kathy walked to the French doors and then turned around to view the three walls from a different angle. "So, Sidney, tell me what happens in this room, exactly. Give me some details."

"Well, Kathy. I could 'tell' you, but we're going to learn by doing. Let's take the next 90 minutes to create 'Superior Dental.'" Sidney grabbed a fat black marker and wrote 'Superior Dental' in the middle of the central white wall.

Like kids in a toy store they got to work. Carl, Kathy, Vinny, Steve, Sergio and Sidney brainstormed and painted a 3D plan for Superior Dental. They played with multiple branding ideas for signage and messaging and added their core values with definitions. A purpose, vision, mission were crafted. They talked and composed elements of infrastructure with help from Sergio. They put questions on Post-Its and stuck them on the white walls where they didn't have answers. They created a website, using the index cards to indicate pages and links and resources. When they ran out of room on the central white board, they expanded to the side walls, connecting ideas by affixing colorful string to magnets between them.

In short order they had puzzled together a physical abstract of a group practice. Standing on the far side of the work table they admired their work, but they also marveled at how the pieces Sidney and

Sergio had been talking about all fit together. It provided a deeper understanding of the components of group practice in a way that listening alone hadn't. They were proud, surprised, and connected to each other in a new, more meaningful way. They had created this 'thing' together. They had collaborated and compromised and brainstormed life into Superior Dental.

When they were done, Sidney pulled out his iPhone and, starting at the outside corner of the left-hand white wall, took a panoramic picture that ended at the outside corner of the right-hand board so they would have a single photo of the 'map' to have and share and remember.

Right about noon, Dawn came in with a festive tray of wine glasses filled with cold hard apple cider from a local Santa Fe brewery. They toasted, they laughed and they wholeheartedly appreciated their work laying out 'Superior Dental.' Periodically, someone would add a question on a Post-It and stick it somewhere on one of the three walls.

Sidney congratulated them on their work in taking an abstract vision and quickly outlining the nuts and bolts to concretize it. "I couldn't say for sure when we came up with the idea of this room, but it works. This kind of collaboration among dentists is the future of dentistry."

CHAPTER 26

By the time they returned to the Great Room, the large screen monitor had been set up behind the couch farthest from the fireplace with the picture Sidney had taken just moments earlier. Three walls of the White Room with the bones of Superior Dental scratched out.

Sidney started. "I hope this exercise helped you get a clearer picture of *one type* of group practice. Anyone have thoughts on the process?"

Steve raised his hand and spoke. "You know, this whole process has been tough for me. I didn't want to have to deal with this change in practice. There's still a part of me resisting it and I'm not exactly sure how I'll move forward. But, in the Thinking Map Room, working with a group of docs, I got a feeling that maybe it's not an *impossible* thing to do. This trip to Taos has been eye-opening. I wasn't prepared to enjoy it, so I appreciate you all putting up with my skepticism. I'm still not completely sold, but my mind is much more open."

Sidney smiled. "We both knew that this was not a direction you particularly wanted to go, and still you came. The purpose of this workshop is to open your eyes and mind to the possibility—and growing necessity—of group practice. I'm glad at least that there's another option before you now."

"I want to thank you, too, Sidney," Kathy said. "I've never really worked with dentists on anything like we just did with the Thinking Map white boards. It was invigorating. I feel like I have new best friends and partners in my future. Superior Dental feels like something more tangible now. And not because it's in this photo, but because all of you jumped in to breathe life into it. I think we all have similar core values and beliefs about our profession and want to create something bigger and more profound with our skills."

Vinny nodded. "I agree, Kathy. Wholeheartedly. There was a synergy in the room, I felt, and it got me to thinking 'who' in my community would be that kind of partner in crime, you know? And how I could create my own Superior Dental in Philly. Like, Cheese Steak Dental, maybe?"

The group shared a good laugh.

"Well, I'm glad your experience in the Thinking Map Room was useful. If we can generate a Superior Dental and a Cheese Steak Dental in less than two hours, then no telling what else is possible," Sidney told them. "Maybe that social archeologist I mentioned yesterday will see the dental timeline branch out in unexpected ways. Any thoughts you want to share, Carl?"

"Sure. I've been riding the fence pretty hard up to now. I think, like Steve, I was just afraid of this change and used my need for more detail as a foil against deciding. Kathy, you're amazing in your embrace of the group idea and I know that if I were to throw my lot in with you, and possibly Jim Boomer, it would be a thrilling ride.

"When we were with Richard at the bonfire last night, with the drums and tambourines, I learned to let go. Today in the Thinking Map Room was like that, too. I guess I've been so stressed and worried about the future of my practice, and my family, that I wasn't able to relax. I feel much more relieved and focused now. I can't tell you how much I appreciate what you've done for us, Sidney and Sergio."

"Thanks, Carl." Sidney replied. "I don't expect everyone to rush off and start a group, but it's very satisfying to know that you've come away with a renewed feeling about your profession and your future in it."

Sergio added, "We know it takes a lot of work. Hard work. But if you can assemble a team of professionals who all want it to work, then you forge a common future, you abide by the same values, you become like family."

"As Sergio said it's a lot of hard work and we are here to help if you commit to a group practice. You really have three choices as you return to your homes. One, keep what you have and fight to make it work. Two, find a group that will buy you and become part of that group. Or three, generate your own group. What you choose is totally up to you. If you decide a group practice is the way to go, I have coaches I can recommend to help you get started on the process.

"Before we have lunch and you get packed up and on the road, please share one word that encapsulates our time together this weekend."

"Energized," Kathy said.

"Revived," Carl said.

"Cheese Steak Dental," Vinny said with a grin.

"Thank goodness I don't live in Philadelphia," Steve said and then added, "Awakened."

Sidney shook each of their hands. "I hope the bonds of friendship you've all come away with stick and that you all will support each in any direction you decide to go. Alright, let's break bread together one last time over one of Dawn's fabulous meals."

CHAPTER 27

As they waited for Richard, Carl and Kathy made arrangements with Sergio for a visit to tour his practice in Houston. They planned to first meet up with Jim Boomer to gauge his interest and then set a date not too far off.

Sidney joined them and passed out large white padded envelopes to the four doctors. Kathy opened hers to find a print of the Thinking Map Room picture, enclosed in a clear, acrylic case with the date at the bottom. "I hope this will serve to remind you that anything is possible."

"Sidney, you sure make it feel that way," Kathy said. "Thanks for everything."

"You know this means we'll be leaning on your wisdom the next few years," Carl told Sidney.

"You know, it's not about me, Carl. It's always about you. Trusting yourself and your values. Give Veronica my best."

Richard rolled up in the white van and jumped out to load suitcases.

Carl ended up in the front seat. "You know, Richard, I think I prefer the old pickup after all."

"Guess, I'll have to play some good ol' country and western music to give you a feel for it," Richard said.

"Bring it on," Carl dared.

Richard tuned the radio and a Zac Brown Band song came on called *Quiet Your Mind:*

I feel the change
Goin' on all around me
It's strange
How I'm taken and guided
Where I end up right I'm needed to be

Quiet your mind
Soak it all in
It's a game you can't win
Enjoy the ride

Carl sat back and listened to the lyrics trying to soak in all he'd experience at the ranch. He thought about Veronica and home. He was excited to tell her everything about the possibility of practicing as a group with Kathy and Jim Boomer.

Like the first time he'd come to Taos, he was leaving New Mexico with a renewed sense of purpose and the desire to grow and see his practice benefit from everything he had learned. He had little doubt that the staff would embrace the group idea. The group model made sense, it was laden with upside and he knew they could really make a difference in their profession and in the communities of the 'golden triangle.'

It was time to enjoy the ride.

"How's that music sitting with you, Carl," Richard asked. And then he grinned.

Carl smiled wide in return. "Starting to enjoy the ride, Fierce Eagle. Finally, enjoying the ride."

The long, wide road ahead looked clear and inviting.

−Festina Lente−

SUPERIOR DENTAL
YEAR: 2020

Superior Dental LLC was initially formed with the merger of three Wisconsin dental practices. Superior Dental is one of the most successful and highly considered multi-specialty dental groups in the Great Lakes region with dentists specializing in general dentistry, pedodontics, orthodontics, endodontics, periodontics, cosmetic dentistry, restorative, and oral surgery.

Today Superior Dental has 27 Dental Care Centers and 5 Emergency Dental Units located adjacent to hospitals with 116 dentists and 302 dental support staff providing dental care services throughout the region.

Superior Dental is committed to providing the highest quality care available. Technology, materials, highly trained dental healthcare professionals, service support and access are all key components to providing the best care to the most people as efficiently and economically as possible. Superior Dental provides 'concierge' level services to every patient.

VISION

Provide the most extraordinary dental healthcare available that supports overall health and well-being for every patient.

MISSION

Create a network of dental facilities that are value-driven, outcomes-based, and committed to excellent patient service; doing the right care at the right time at the right cost; operated by premiere dentists who are anchored to the communities they serve.

PURPOSE

Generate a multi-specialty, multi-location enterprise that is value motivated, quality driven, and outcomes and evidence-based determined.

DR. MARC B. COOPER

Dr. Cooper is President and CEO of The Mastery Company. He has been a consultant to the health care industry for over 30 years—at the practice management level as well as corporate and organizational levels. Prior to his consulting career, Dr. Cooper was an academician, basic science researcher and practicing periodontist.

The Mastery Company has been in existence since 1984. Dr. Cooper's client experience in dentistry includes solo private practice, small partnered practices, managed group practices and retail corporate enterprises. Dr. Cooper has worked with numbers of health care entities such as insurance companies, clearing houses, bio-technical companies and disease management companies, as well as the senior executives and boards of large hospitals and hospital systems and a number of their related physician groups.

Dr. Cooper currently lives on a houseboat in Portland, Oregon.

CHRIS CREAMER

Chris Creamer has worked as managing partner of the Mastery Company, a small dental consultancy, for twenty years. Prior to his work with the Mastery Company, Mr. Creamer worked with a company that designed and delivered corporate training events for Fortune 500 companies all across the U.S.

Mr. Creamer directs and coordinates technology initiatives, all multimedia development projects, operations, as well as every aspect of branding for The Mastery Company. He was instrumental in co-developing The Mastery Company's suite of online surveys and assessments used by clients to evaluate all aspects of their business performance.

Mr. Creamer currently resides in Woodinville, Washington, the epicenter of Washington State's wine industry, has been married for twenty-four years and has two children in college.

Sahalie Press
PO Box 1806
Woodinville WA 98072

The Mastery Company
MasteryCompany.com
info@MasteryCompany.com

www.ingramcontent.com/pod-product-compliance
Lightning Source LLC
Chambersburg PA
CBHW020426220526
45464CB00002B/586